LANGUAGE
AND READING
SUCCESS

by

Andrew Biemiller

University of Toronto

Volume 5 in the series
From Reading Research to Practice

Brookline Books

Dedication

I dedicate this book to the teachers and children of Rose Avenue Public School, Toronto, and the Laboratory School of the Institute of Child Study, University of Toronto, who have taught me much of what I know about the relationship between language and reading.

Acknowledgments

Without the support and encouragement of Jeanne Chall, this book would not have been written. I also wish to thank the Humanities and Social Science Research Council of Canada and the Government of Ontario for their ongoing support of my work on language and reading.

ISBN 1-57129-068-0

Library of Congress Cataloging-In-Publication Data
(to come)

Book design and typography by Erica L. Schultz.

Printed in USA
10 9 8 7 6 5 4 3 2 1

Published by
BROOKLINE BOOKS
P.O. Box 1047
Cambridge, Massachusetts 02238
Order toll-free: 1-800-666-BOOK

Contents

Preface

In a field where conflicting views on best practices are all too common, it is comforting to know that there is almost complete agreement on the relation between language skills and reading skills. All researchers acknowledge that language is necessary for full development of reading and that growth in reading, in turn, benefits language development.

Andrew Biemiller's *Language and Reading Success* brings to teachers the important research, theories, and effective practices on the nature of this relationship. He highlights how the relationship changes from the preschool through the elementary grades and how the teacher can enhance the growth of each, and hence, the development of the other.

In this short, readable book, he provides valuable information on such topics as vocabulary development for reading and language, readability standards that are most useful for language and reading development, and how to assess vocabulary difficulty in books.

The reading teacher will find this book a treasure trove of research and practical information for immediate use in the classroom.

Jeanne S. Chall, Ph.D., *Series Editor*
John F. Onofrey, *Editor*

Chapter One

Language and Reading Success

To succeed at reading, a child must be able to *identify* or "read" printed words and to *understand* the story or text composed of those words. Both identifying words and understanding text are critical to reading success. Many books in this series focus on the identification of printed words. This book focuses on understanding *language*. For many children, increasing reading and school success will involve increasing oral language competence in the elementary years.

The main argument of this book runs as follows:

- During elementary school, at any given time, a child's maximum level of reading comprehension is determined by the child's level of listening comprehension.[1]
- Children differ markedly in the language and especially the vocabulary they have upon entering kindergarten. Advanced children (75th percentile) are about a "year" ahead of average children, while delayed children (25th percentile) are about a year behind. (Bankson, 1977; Dunn, 1982).
- Language continues to develop during the primary years. *However, the gap between children with advanced language and children with restricted language grows wider during the elementary years.* By grade 3, advanced children's comprehension is equivalent to that of average children in grade 4 while slower-progressing children are similar to average second graders or even younger children. Some of this difference is attributable to *cumulative vocabulary deficits* in less advanced children.
- *Current school practices typically have little effect on oral language development during the primary years.*[2] Because the level of language used is often lim-

---

[1] Later, adolescents and adults may comprehend more complex printed narrative or expository text than spoken text because print remains after reading and can be reviewed, while oral language usually cannot be reviewed. However, children must reach the point where they can understand printed text as well as spoken text before their comprehension of printed text can exceed their comprehension of spoken text.

[2] This is true for children whose first language is English. Non-English-speaking children in English-speaking schools clearly acquire some English. However, as a group, they also clearly remain at a disadvantage compared to English-speaking children in elementary schools.

ited to what the children can read and write, there are few opportunities for language development in primary classes.

- In the upper elementary grades, *those who enter fourth grade with significant vocabulary deficits show increasing problems with reading comprehension*, even if they have good reading (word identification) skills. The available evidence does not suggest a substantial "catching-up" process, but rather a continuing slippage relative to those with average and above-average achievement.

- Thus early delays in oral language come to be reflected in low levels of reading comprehension, leading to low levels of academic success. Clearly, if we are to increase children's ability to profit from education, we will have to enrich their oral language development during the early years of schooling. Although not all differences in language are due to differences in opportunity and learning, *schools could clearly do much more than they do now to foster the language development of less advantaged children, and children for whom English is a second language.* The main purposes of this book are to examine the need for fostering higher levels of language development and to suggest some ways of doing so.

In this book, I will consider the evidence for each these propositions. In this chapter, I will look at the relationship between comprehending spoken language and comprehending written language, as well as individual differences in language development and specific data on the growth of vocabulary. In Chapter Two, I will examine language and vocabulary development before school. I will particularly emphasize the ranges of language and vocabulary development. I will also consider what is known about influences on early language development. Chapter Three will focus on language development during the elementary years, the minimal impact of schooling on language growth, and the growth of "cumulative vocabulary deficits." In Chapter Four, I will consider some effective language curricula at the kindergarten and primary level.

In Chapter Five, I will consider some effective language curricula for the upper elementary grades. Teachers presently carry a tremendous load in elementary school. How can an additional focus on oral language development be accommodated in the primary years? How can an additional focus on vocabulary acquisition and strategies for dealing with new words be accommodated in the upper elementary grades? In Chapter Six, I look at what is needed in educational programs to ensure that more children develop language to their potential. I also examine some barriers to an increasing emphasis on language development, and some possible solutions.

The Relationship Between Listening and Reading Comprehension

Although there has been a good deal of research on the relationship between listening and reading comprehension (Sticht & James, 1984), there is little research directly contrasting children's achievement using the same comprehension measures for both listening and reading comprehension. Mary Elizabeth Curtis (1980) carried out one such study; her findings for average (grade level) children are described in a simplified fashion in Figure 1 below.

The listening comprehension of the average child begins to develop around twelve months of age and continues to grow long after grade 6. Reading comprehension typically begins to develop in kindergarten or first grade. At this point, the child's level of reading comprehension is obviously far below her listening comprehension. There is considerable evidence that for the majority of children, comprehension of printed language continues to lag behind com-

Figure 1: Listening and reading comprehension by grade.

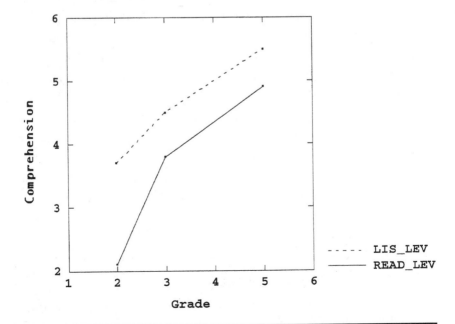

prehension of spoken language well past third grade (Sticht & James, 1984). *When a child can understand language equally well whether presented in print or speech, the distinction between listening and reading comprehension ceases to be important.* However, a number of studies suggest that *average* children don't reach the point of being able to read anything they could understand if they heard it until around seventh or eighth grade.[3]

There is a strong relationship between the early growth of vocabulary and later reading competence. For example, Cunningham and Stanovich (1997) have found that reading comprehension tested in eleventh grade could be predicted to a considerable degree (technically, about 50%) from listening vocabulary known in first grade (Peabody Picture Vocabulary Test). We cannot tell from these data to what extent this relationship reflects differences in early and continuing *opportunities* to build vocabulary and language versus early and continuing *talent* for learning language. (I will address that issue in Chapters Two and Three.) But we can see that the state of vocabulary early in one's education has some bearing on later achievement.

Listening comprehension continues to grow during the elementary years. Thus the typical third-grader can comprehend more complex oral stories, expositions, etc., than the typical first-grader. Broadly speaking, language can only "grow" through interaction with people and texts which introduce new vocabulary, concepts, and language structures. In grades 1 to 3, this growth *cannot* result mainly from reading experiences because most children are not reading content that is as advanced as their oral language. For many children, listening comprehension continues to be more advanced than reading comprehension through eighth grade or later. We often assume that children's reading experiences contribute much to their increasing ability to comprehend language (e.g., Nagy & Herman, 1987; Sternberg, 1987). However, the information on listening comprehension presented here suggests that for many children, most language growth continues to come from non-print sources (parents, peers, teacher lectures, class discussions, television, etc.) *throughout the elementary years.* For many children, the skills necessary for reading printed English remain too poor for them to read texts that introduce new vocabulary and new conceptual structures.

---

[3] Of course they can understand simpler text sooner. Many second graders can read and understand "first grade" written text. But they cannot understand stories and expository material in print that they can understand when heard.

Individual Differences in the Growth of Comprehension of Spoken and Printed Language

Figure 1 showed the development of spoken and written language comprehension for *average* children. What happens to the majority of children, whose language development is either well above or well below average? Figure 2 below shows the development of listening vocabulary of children at the 75th and 25th percentiles.[4] (Figure 2 is based on the norms of the Peabody Picture Vocabulary Test.)

Figure 2 shows that by age 12 (grade 6), the listening vocabulary level of the 25th percentile child is equivalent to that attained by the 75th percentile child almost 3 years earlier (grade 3). The same is true of reading comprehension measures. Of course, differences are even greater for children above the 75th or below the 25th percentiles. (By definition, nearly *50%* of children are either above the 75th percentile, or below the 25th.)

If we could improve the reading (word identification) skills of children at

Figure 2: 25th and 75th percentile vocabulary by age.

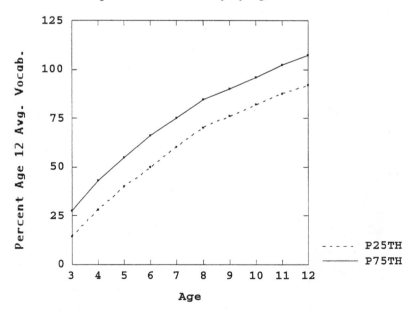

---

[4] "Percentiles" refer to one's performance relative to others. In this instance, children at the 75th percentile comprehended *more* complex language than 74 percent of their age mates. Children at the 25th percentile comprehended *less* complex language than 74 percent of their classmates.

the 25th percentile in reading comprehension, we would get some improvement — up to the child's *listening* comprehension level. But in many cases, we would still be looking at a child whose comprehension level is far below that of many peers. Especially after grade 2, many children at the 25th percentile in reading comprehension have *language* comprehension levels that are too low to profit from independent reading of most "grade-level" textbooks (Chall & Conard, 1991). Put simply, they lack the vocabulary needed to understand grade-level texts, even if they can identify the printed words.

Children appear to learn words in a roughly similar order. For example, it is possible to identify certain words as commonly learned by age 8, while others are not commonly learned before age 10. It is also the case that words typically learned by advanced children at age 8 will tend to be those learned by less advanced children by age 10. This phenomenon is known as "developmental stability" (Bloom, 1964). To illustrate, I have found a quite similar order of word knowledge development in a sample of advantaged upper-middle-class children, and a sample of relatively disadvantaged children whose home language is not English (English as a Second Language or ESL children). The correlation between how well words are known by advantaged third-graders and by ESL sixth-graders is over r = .70 (Biemiller, unpublished data). To the extent that vocabulary growth follows a predictable course, it becomes possible for us to specify a vocabulary-ordered curriculum — one which ensures opportunities to acquire most of the root words commonly acquired at particular ages or in a particular order.

The Relationship Between Comprehension, Passage Difficulty, and Vocabulary. For practical purposes, what we call "comprehension" is the ability to answer reasonable questions about a passage one has heard or read. A child's ability to answer comprehension test questions is determined in part by the knowledge of the child, and in part by the difficulty of the passage. (Of course, in the case of *reading* comprehension, the child's ability to easily identify the printed words is also necessary.) Both child knowledge and passage difficulty reflect *vocabulary*. Thus a child comprehending at grade level turns out to have a grade-level vocabulary. In fact, the correlation between print vocabulary test performance and reading comprehension is generally in the .70 to .80 range (Bloom, 1976). Conversely, determining that a passage is at a particular grade level or readability level is generally done by assessing the vocabulary demands of the passage. For example, in the Dale-Chall readability formula, passages with roughly 15% of hard words (words not known by 80% of fourth-graders)

are identified as fourth-grade passages (understood by ?
Passages with more than 20% of words not known by ʃ
fied as sixth-grade passages.[5] Put more simply, as a chʲ
ability to understand progressively more difficult teː
(1991) and Fry (1989) provide direct evidence of the sʰ.
tween reading comprehension achievement scores and readabıⁿ.
to a considerable degree, vocabulary *knowledge* (including a grasp of tⁱ.
ings denoted by words) determines language comprehension and literacy.

Thus, to bring a child to grade-level language comprehension means at a minimum
that the child must acquire and use grade-level vocabulary plus some post-grade level
vocabulary. Obviously, this does not mean simply memorizing more words, but
rather coming to understand and use the words used by average children at that
level. Knowledge of this vocabulary will not guarantee success, but lack of
knowledge of vocabulary can ensure failure. This conclusion is supported by
the strong correlations found between vocabulary and comprehension achievement (Bloom, 1976; Beck & McKeown, 1991), and in the evidence that comprehension performance is reduced when test passages contain 10–20% uncom-
mon or pseudowords (Freebody & Anderson, 1983; Marks, Doctorow, &
Wittrock, 1974; , Wittrock, Marks, & Doctorow, 1975). In later chapters, I will
examine possible ways of bringing lower-achieving children to more advanced
levels of language and vocabulary.

The Growth of Vocabulary

There have been many studies attempting to specify the size and range of vocabulary at different ages. Surprisingly, these vary tremendously in the sizes of
vocabulary reported. For example, Templin (1957) reports an average vocabulary of 14,000 words by the beginning of grade 1, while Dupuy (1973) reports
about 1,000 words at the same point.

Much of the difference among researchers' vocabulary counts is due to
what they treat as a "word." At one extreme, Templin counts all syntactic and
semantic variations of words (e.g., *word, words, worded, wordy, re-word, non-word,*
wordless, etc.) as separate "words." She also counts proper nouns. At the oppo-
site extreme, Dupuy sought to identify only "root words" (e.g., only *word* in the

---

[5] This holds for passages with average sentence lengths of 15 words or less. Grade levels increase for
passages with longer sentences. The evidence supporting these readability ratings is performance
on comprehension tests and performance on cloze tests (children's ability to guess a proportion of
words deleted from a text). See Chall and Dale (1995).

eliminating all grammatical and semantic variations (plurals, tenses, such as *un-*, suffixes such as *-less*), compound words, and idioms. It is ~~~at the largest estimates of vocabulary (e.g., Templin, 1957, or M.K. Smith, ~~~) substantially exaggerate actual vocabulary sizes (Lorge & Chall, 1963).[6] ~~~any researchers attempt to identify a middle ground of "psychologically basic words" — those which are probably *learned* when they are encountered rather than *derived* or "figured out" from their components. My own preference is to focus on these "basic words" — words which must be *learned* to become a literate or "educated" member of our society, but to give special emphasis to "root words" and powerful affixes (prefixes and suffixes) which combine with root words to greatly extend vocabulary.

Probably the best recent vocabulary growth data comes from a study by Jeremy Anglin (1993). His findings, based on a sample of English-speaking children from a wide range of backgrounds, suggest that between grades 1 and 5, the average total vocabulary increases from 10,000 to 40,000 words! However, when this is restricted to root words and idioms, words that must be learned, vocabulary increases from 3200 in grade 1 to 5200 in grade 3 and to 10,000 root words and idioms in grade 5.[7]

Edgar Dale and Joseph O'Rourke's *Living Word Vocabulary* is an excellent source of vocabulary data (1981). This book contains a listing of words used in public school along with the grade level at which these words are known by 67-80% of the students surveyed. Dale and O'Rourke show roughly 2,500 *root words* known by grade 2, rising to 5,000 by grade 4, 7,600 by grade 6, 10,700 by grade 8 and 14,800 by grade 12. *Idioms* represent another 130 words at grade 2, rising to 1,000 by grade 6 and 2,600 by grade 12.[8] (The distinction between *root words* and *idioms* is an important one. In this book, I am going to emphasize the importance of learning *root* words (e.g., *happy*) — which typically lead to knowledge of many "derived" words (e.g., *unhappy, happiness, happier*) — rather than idioms (e.g., *doubting Thomas*) which typically are unique terms. These

---

6 The reasons for this are quite technical. See Lorge and Chall (1963).

7 In Chapter Three, I will return to the issue of words that are "learned" versus words that can be known on the basis of their components.

8 Dale and O'Rourke report roughly twice this number of words known at each age level. The determination of numbers of root words and idioms is based on a sampling of 100 words at each grade level, using Anglin's (1993) criteria. Dale and O'Rourke identify words at a "grade level" if 67-80% of children at that level "know" the word. However, their data is based on unadjusted results from three-alternative multiple choice tests. Adjusted for guessing, these come to 50-70% of children knowing words well enough to pick the correct alternative. The "grade 2" words are words known by more than 80% of grade 4 children.

figures are reasonably close to those determined by Anglin. Furthermore, the correlation between the rank of difficulty of the sample of words used in Anglin's study and the "grade level" of those same words in Dale and O'Rourke's dictionary is r = .78.

For practical purposes, we can conclude that there are about 5,000 root words which need to be acquired and used by the time children complete grade 4. They should also acquire some more advanced words. Three thousand of these grade 2–4 words are identified in Chall and Dale's (1995) book on readability assessment. Examination of this list suggests that few of these words represent difficult concepts. My own research tentatively suggests that about half of these words may be known even by disadvantaged children. (A list of these words is provided in Appendix A, indicating which words are more likely to require instructional support.)[9] A substantial proportion of children at the fourth-grade level know many more advanced words (Biemiller, 1998). However, it appears to be a reasonable goal to ensure that by grade 4 most children should be able to use and understand *at least* the basic vocabulary of 4,000 to 5,000 words, and that they are adding vocabulary at a normal rate.

To add vocabulary "at a normal rate" would require roughly 1,200 *root* words per school year, or 6 per school day,[10] prior to grade 4. Preliminary studies suggest that most children are learning at least half of these words independently of any special effort by schools. Thus adding 2 to 4 new root words per day through planned school activities would be sufficient to ensure normal vocabulary growth, assuming we can correctly determine which words would be learned anyway. This also assumes that children will be acquiring the necessary *morphological* or "word analytic" skills to interpret "derived" words (e.g., *wordless, non-word, undemocratic*). Anglin's (1993) data suggests that many or most children are acquiring these morphological skills.

It could be argued that what is important is knowing "advanced" words (that is, those known by older children, or words representing cognitively more complex concepts). I suspect that it may be more important simply to be familiar with *most* of the words one is likely to encounter in the course of speaking or reading, and that the best guide to such words are lists of words known by most children at particular ages. I have already cited evidence that comprehension suffers when 5–15% of words in a passage are unknown. The only way to

---

9   This list is based on the level of accuracy at which these words were known at grade 4. Those above the 90% level were considered highly familiar. Those below 90% were considered less likely to be known. This assumption is supported empirically in the case of a sample of 60 of the words.

10 Based on 180 school days per year.

ensure that most words in a passage will be known is to use words already known, or to provide word knowledge support while children are reading or listening. The current reality is that neither of these conditions are met for many students. We will return to this question in Chapter Six.

Conclusion

In this chapter, we have looked at how listening comprehension sets an upper limit to reading comprehension, at how assessment of both individual levels of comprehension and the "comprehensibility" of texts are determined by vocabulary, and at the growth of vocabulary. I concluded that it would be desirable for most children to be familiar with the words now known by half to two-thirds of children. Let us now turn to what is known about the early growth of language — before school, and at the role schooling currently plays in promoting language development.

Chapter Two

Language Development Before School

By the time children begin kindergarten, they have already acquired much of their language. They speak in sentences, and they understand simple narratives and simple expository language. Most probably know more than one thousand root words.

However, there are substantial differences in language achievement among children at the beginning of kindergarten. How do these differences come about? Age differences alone have a substantial impact. The youngest kindergartners are 20% younger than the oldest kindergartners.[11] There are also substantial differences in language and vocabulary associated with social class, and obviously children growing up in a non-English-speaking family are at a disadvantage. Let us consider briefly the range of language differences at the beginning of school, the developmental nature of language growth, and some of the early influences on language growth.

Range of Language Development at the Beginning of Kindergarten

Norms for the Bankson Language Test (which assesses vocabulary, grammar, memory, and a bit of comprehension) show that children in the 25th percentile are a year behind the median at age 5, and will not reach the language level of advanced 5-year-old children (75th percentile) until they are 6 (Bankson, 1977). As noted above, both the normal differences between children of the *same* age, and the 12-month range of age found in kindergarten play a role here. According to the Peabody Vocabulary Test norms, a "young" kindergartner who is just under 5 years old when beginning kindergarten would have to be in the 86th percentile to have the *same* absolute vocabulary as an average (50th percentile) "old" kindergarten child who is just under 6 years old,. Thus a slower-develop-

---

[11] Some jurisdictions also offer "junior" or four-year-old kindergarten programs.

ing "young" kindergartner is even more disadvantaged in comparison with a rapidly developing "old" kindergartner.

Early Influences on Language Growth

Is it simply the case that some children have been advantaged by heredity and that this accounts for observed differences? Alternatively, is it simply the case that some children have been advantaged by circumstances — by the family, community, and education system in which they grow up, and that this accounts for observed differences? It is clear that both constitutional differences in children (*nature*) and differences in children's experience (*nurture*) have substantial impacts on how rapidly a child's language develops. Indeed, the relationship between listening vocabulary and many of the other skills measured on "intelligence tests" is so strong that vocabulary measures are sometimes treated as intelligence tests.[12] On the other hand, there is clear evidence that variations in children's environment are associated with marked differences in language and vocabulary development, and that fairly simple interventions can double normal vocabulary growth rates (to be discussed in Chapter Four). Language development does not simply follow a biologically programmed schedule. Let us consider briefly some of the factors influencing language and vocabulary growth.

Constitutional Factors. To learn words easily, one must be able to form what I call "phonological files" easily, files that allow a person to readily remember and reproduce the *sound* of a novel word. In addition, one must develop "referent connections" to which the word-sound *refers*. These referent concepts (or "collections of connections," as Miller, 1991, describes them) must either form easily or already be extant when a "word" is learned. For example, an infant may already have an mental "file" about cups when she first learns the word *cup*.[13] Learning the meaning of the word *cup* simply involves connecting the word-sound with the pre-existing nonverbal "file" on cups. On the other hand, when the word *fair* is learned, a complex referent concept regarding "fair" and "unfair" transactions is probably gradually constructed. It is unlikely that a

---

[12] On the other hand, about half of what is measured on the standard IQ test is verbal in nature — thus, to some extent saying that vocabulary reflects intelligence is tautological.

[13] This may be circular. In an address to the Society for the Scientific Study of Reading, Alvin Liberman (1998, April) suggested that the development of phonological skill may rest in part on the acquisition of a large number of words. Gathercole, Hitch, Service, and Martin (1997) also support this view.

nonverbal "file" on fairness exists prior to encountering *fair* in verbal interaction. (A completely different referent concept regarding "fairs" as a social setting is also learned at some point.)

There are probably constitutional factors affecting the ease both of forming phonological files and of developing referent files and connections. Thus it is not surprising that young children with a strong command of word sounds develop larger vocabularies than comparable children with less strong phonological skills (Gathercole, Hitch, Service, & Martin, 1997). In addition, "working memory," a general cognitive capacity necessary for word formation, is also implicated in language development. One must be able to think about a word and its meaning at the same time (Case, 1985; Gathercole et al., 1997). More generally, the growth of working memory seems to underlie basic conceptual development (Case, 1985; Case & Okamoto, 1998). Thus progress through the various stages of cognitive development has been shown to be closely associated with the growth of working memory. This is likely to influence the mental or cognitive "level" of words learned, in addition to the ease of learning specific words.

Much more could be said of constitutional factors influencing language growth, but these examples should be sufficient to establish that such factors have an effect. To a large extent, the effect of constitutional factors is to increase or decrease the *rate* or *ease* of word learning. In short, there is reasonable evidence for the existence of a constitutionally-based "talent" for learning words and language. However, the number of words learned, (and other language structures developed) will be influenced by a combination of this learning rate and the *opportunities* children encounter for learning language.

Experiential Factors. It is not news that children who grow up in low-income/poorly educated families are likely to have smaller vocabularies and less advanced language development than their more advantaged peers (research extensively summarized in McLloyd, 1998; Duncan, Brooks-Gunn, & Klebanov, 1994). These differences are clearly apparent by the time children start school. However, social class, as indexed by family income and education, is a gross index for what must be a combination of specific family and community child-rearing practices plus some possible group differences in constitutional cognitive potential. I have already discussed constitutional differences which may affect the rate of language development. Let us now turn to child-rearing practices and opportunities that may also affect language development. What is different about the home environments of disadvantaged children?

Betty Hart and Todd Risley (1995) have written what may be the clearest book describing language and achievement differences between advantaged and disadvantaged children, and differences in their early experiences. By age three, advantaged children were found to have twice the vocabulary of welfare children, and were adding vocabulary at twice the rate (6 words/day vs. 3 words/day). The vocabulary measure was correlated with the children's IQ (r = .70, Stanford-Binet). (The "IQ" measure is itself in part a measure of vocabulary.) However, vocabulary was even more strongly correlated with a measure of parent interaction combining (a) different words per hour, (b) feedback tone or warmth on interaction, (c) "symbolic emphasis,"[14] (d) "guidance style" (directive vs. suggestive), and (e) "responsiveness" (proportion of parent responses to child-initiated talk) (r = .78). Hart and Risley summarized their overall observations of differences in children's language-related experience:

> To illustrate the differences in the amount of children's language experience using numbers, rather than just "more" and "less," we can derive an estimate based simply on words heard per hour. The longitudinal data showed that in the everyday interactions at home, the average (rounded) number of words children heard per hour was 2,150 in the professional families, 1,250 in the working-class families, and 620 in the welfare families. ... Given the consistency we saw in the data, we might venture to extrapolate to the first 3 years of life. By age 3 the children in professional families would have heard more than 30 million words, the children in working class families 20 million words, and the children in welfare families 10 million. ...
>
> In professional families the extraordinary amount of talk, the many different words, and the greater richness of nouns, modifiers, and past-tense verbs suggest a culture concerned with symbols and analytic problem solving. To ensure their children access to advanced education, parents spent time and effort developing their children's potential, asking questions, and using affirmatives to encourage their children to listen, to notice how words refer and relate, and to practice the distinctions to be made among them. Effort meant attending closely to what their children said and did and adapting talk promptly and adroitly in order to challenge and guide exploration. Especially important was keeping their children engaged with adults, and practicing language in the presence of more skilled models of the culture.
>
> In the welfare families, the lesser amount of talk with its more frequent parent-initiated topics, imperatives, and prohibitions suggested a culture con-

---

[14] An index of the relative frequency of nouns, modifiers, and past-tense verbs among all parental words directed to the child.

cerned with established customs. To teach socially acceptable behavior, language rich in nouns and modifiers was not called for; obedience, politeness, and conformity were more likely to be the keys to survival. Rather than attempting to prepare their children with the knowledge and skills required in a technological world with which the parents had had little experience, parents seemed to be preparing their children realistically for jobs likely to be open to them, jobs in which success and advancement would be determined by attitude, how well the children presented themselves, and whether they could prove themselves through their performance.

Among the working class families we saw a mixture of these cultures. We saw upwardly mobile families in which the parents named, prompted, and tested with all the intensity and adaptability of the professional parents and at the same time used imperatives and prohibitions to convey expectations for obedience and conformity similar to those of the welfare parents. We saw one parent take time from a job and a large family to intervene for an intense 3 months of prompting the child to name, relate, recall, and describe. Another parent often used imperatives and prohibitions to demand appropriate behavior: paying attention to the words on *Sesame Street*.

[*Source:* Hart, B., & Risley, T. (1995). *Meaningful Differences in the Everyday Experience of Young American Children* (pp. 131-134). Baltimore: Paul H. Brookes.]

Similar findings exist in other observational studies. In Gordon Wells's study of language in the home, a significant correlation was found between total adult talk to children and the quality and gains over time in children's language. Larger correlations were found between gains in child language and the percentage of adult talk that involved extensions of child language (Wells, 1985, p. 391). Burton White's famous study contrasting the home environment of advantaged and disadvantaged children similarly indicated marked differences in the dialogue directed to children (White & Watts, 1973).[15] In general, children develop language more rapidly in homes where parents (usually mothers) seriously engage in dialogue with their language-learning preschoolers.[16]

---

[15] For more information, see L. Bloom (1998, pp. 334ff); Snow (1995); Bates, Dale, & Thal (1995).

[16] In the present era, more than half of preschoolers and infants are partially raised by caretakers other than parents. Unfortunately, I am aware of no observational studies that begin to contrast the quality of language interaction between caretakers and children with the qualities of mother-child interaction observed in upper-, middle-, and lower-SES homes by Todd & Risley, Wells, and White. We do not know *how much* high-level interaction is necessary to promote strong language growth. (We can observe that many "advantaged" children are now largely being raised by caretakers who come from considerably less advantaged backgrounds.)

There is some evidence that this variation occurs independently of socioeconomic (SES) differences. In other words, children develop stronger language when being raised in low-SES circumstances but interacting with their mothers in ways similar to the way high-SES children interact with their mothers.

Language and Experience: Experimental Studies. The preceding studies were all "observational," that is, they describe relationships between observed parent activities and child speech. They do not *prove* that parent behaviors cause more or less language development. It is possible that parents with high language abilities have children with high language abilities and just happen to talk more to their children.

However, a very important study by Barbara Tizard and her colleagues (Tizard et al., 1972) provides strong evidence that what parents and caretakers *"do"* matters — perhaps at least as much as the genetic potential passed on to these children. Tizard and her colleagues studied young children in English residential institutions — orphans or children who had been removed from their parents. They found that the organization of care (i.e., whether care was centrally controlled or was largely the responsibility of a single caregiving nurse) was strongly associated with the level of language development. When an individual nurse was largely responsible for the activities she carried out with a group of six children, she spent more time talking, reading, and playing with her charges, was more "accepting" of the children, took the children on more trips, etc., than when nurses had less responsibility for a specific group and followed centrally-determined procedures. In terms of language, nurses with greater responsibility "offered more informative talk, spoke in longer sentences, gave fewer negative commands, and were more likely to explain themselves when they told the child to do something, than were those in the institutionally oriented groups" (Tizard & Tizard, 1974). Dramatic differences were associated with these rearing conditions. While the nonverbal intelligence of the children in various groups did not differ, mean verbal comprehension among the 18 children in the three most verbally-supportive groups was 1.5 standard deviations higher than the three most institutionally oriented groups — a difference identical to that found between the children of professional families and children of manual workers.

Effects of Reading to Children. Beyond studies of parent-child dialogue are studies of the specific effects of reading to children. In a major review, Bus, Van Izendoorn, & Pellegrini (1995) concluded that reading to children has an average "effect size" of .67 on "language variables" (vocabulary, comprehension).[17] Reading to children had nearly as large an impact on later reading achievement. However, there is considerable variation in reported results, with some studies showing virtually nil effects of reading to children while others report fairly substantial gains. In terms of studies in which vocabulary outcomes were directly assessed, age seems to have been a major factor. The effect of reading to children under 4.5 years old was relatively small (5 studies, mean effect size: .34) while the effect of reading to children 5 to 6 years was substantial (4 studies, mean effect size: .86). Furthermore, we will see in the next chapter that more than "just reading" is required. For children age 5 and over, reading *combined with clarification of unfamiliar vocabulary* is necessary to produce vocabulary gains. For children under 5, it tentatively appears that more elaborate interaction around books may be necessary to demonstrate measurable language gains. It is very likely that reading alone is not enough; children need more general supportive verbal interaction.

I have described the beneficial effects of talking with children and of reading to them when it is combined with intelligent discussion of what is read. The message seems fairly straightforward: children benefit from *interacting* with their parents, not simply being talked *at* or read *to*, but talked *with* and read *with*. This is all very possible for the large majority of English-speaking parents in North America. (Even parents who read poorly should have little difficulty with the books preschoolers enjoy – e.g., books by Richard Scarry, Dr. Seuss, etc.) However, Whitehurst et al. (1994) found it almost impossible to engage disadvantaged parents in reading to their children. They also found it to have little impact, probably because the frequency of parental reading was low. What we don't know is to what extent simpler experiences introducing kindergarten and primary-grade children to language texts with vocabulary assistance can compensate for the lack of earlier intensive language experiences of the types described by Todd and Risley, and by Whitehurst et al.

Summary. Although it is clear that there are some constitutional differences among children in the *rate* at which they learn language, it is equally clear that there are large differences due to the *opportunities presented* to learn and use

---

[17] "Effect size" is an index of effect summarized across a number of studies. An effect size of .67 is equivalent to about 2/3 of a "standard deviation" (a measure of the variation around an average). Typically, about 2/3 of individual cases in a group will not be greater than one standard deviation above or below the average. Thus, a difference between the means of two groups of one standard deviation represents a substantial effect.

language. The dramatic differences in language experienced by advantaged and disadvantaged children in the first five years of life lead to marked differences in their vocabulary and available language structures by the beginning of kindergarten. There is compelling experimental evidence that much of this difference is due to experience, rather than a simple correlate of inherited ability.

English as a Second Language

What about parents (and relatives or other caretakers) in homes where little or no English is spoken? In such homes there are several alternatives — alternatives which are *not* mutually exclusive.

1. Children definitely benefit from being talked and read to in their native language. It is clear that many children who enter kindergarten not speaking English but with a strong knowledge of their parents' language go on to thrive in English. (The editor of this series, Jeanne Chall, is an example.) Research by Cummings (1985) has shown that early strength in one's native language is associated with later school achievement in English.
2. Children may also benefit from planned exposure to English. There is evidence that competence in English assessed at the beginning of first grade predicts competence in reading achievement in English at the end of first grade (Gerlai, 1987).
3. For children whose home language is not English, or whose home provides only limited opportunities to develop language, it is especially important that schools provide increased opportunities for language development in the early childhood years (ages 3 to 8). Unfortunately, as we will see in the next chapter, there is room for concern about the *level of language development opportunities that now exist in many kindergarten and primary-grade programs.*

Conclusion

Some children start school with a smaller vocabulary base than others. As a result of a combination of opportunity and natural rate of word acquisition, they acquire the root words of English more slowly. What happens once children enter school? Does schooling provide more opportunities for expanding the level of listening comprehension? If so, when? We will turn to this question in the next chapter.

Chapter Three

Language Development During Elementary School: The Gap Widens

A wide range of differences in children's language exists when they begin kindergarten. The fact that some of these differences can be related to experiences before kindergarten suggests that schooling can provide an opportunity to *compensate* to some degree for differences in early language experiences in home and child care. Unfortunately, the limited available evidence also suggests that current practices in kindergarten and early primary grades do little to foster vocabulary and language development. In later grades, somewhat more is done to encourage language development. However, evidence suggests that the gap between advantaged and disadvantaged children continues to widen during the elementary years, although this effect is less severe when teachers give more attention to vocabulary and language.

In Chapter One, we saw that the growth of language from grades 1 to 6 involves going from roughly 2000 root words and idioms to over 8000. Growth in vocabulary from grades 1 to 3 *may* be slower than grades 4 to 6 (Anglin, 1993). If the rate is faster in grades 4 to 6, this accelerated rate of vocabulary acquisition is probably due to *reading*, and probably applies only to children whose vocabulary and reading skills are at or above the median.

This chapter is about normal school practices with respect to promoting language development. Chapters Four, Five, and Six will examine experimental and proposed school approaches for improving language development.

We have seen how variations in home experience greatly affect the growth of children's language and vocabulary. This indicates that we *can* initiate policies which promote better language development. For a long time, educators, politicians, and the public at large have believed that schooling provided the best opportunity to "compensate" for variations in home experience. In many school systems, children now begin school or its equivalent at age four (e.g., Head Start, four-year-old kindergarten). In others, the school day for kindergartners has been lengthened to provide more learning opportunities (e.g., full-day kindergarten programs).

However, it may come as a surprise to readers of this book that I will be arguing that *school experience often does little to foster language growth in the early elementary years* (kindergarten to grade 2). In the later elementary years, when greater attention is often given to vocabulary and related skills, cumulative deficits in vocabulary may be too great to be readily overcome.

Vocabulary and Reading Success

Why do I suggest that there is limited opportunity for language growth in the primary years? Let us begin with a story by Wesley Becker. Having implemented a very successful reading program (DISTAR) which resulted in bringing groups of severely disadvantaged children to average or "grade level" performance in first and second grade, Becker found that children from his program "lost ground" in *reading comprehension* to more advanced children in grade 3 (Becker, 1977). "Losing ground" didn't mean becoming less competent, but merely that the children didn't gain competence as fast as "average" children. Becker stressed that as a group these same children did continue to achieve as well as more advantaged children in math. He took this as evidence that the children were capable of learning when taught. He argued that the children's slow progress in reading comprehension reflected a solvable problem of lack of vocabulary, rather than an issue of underlying ability.[18]

When he examined the reading comprehension test used (the Metropolitan Achievement Test), Becker realized that it and other standardized reading comprehension tests showed a marked increase in vocabulary demands starting around third grade. He realized that traditional school basal readers restricted vocabulary to a few hundred words in grade 1 and an additional thousand or less in grade 2. This was done to keep the print word identification load manageable, and to avoid confronting children with new vocabulary while they were acquiring and consolidating print skills (sight-word identification, phonics, use of printed punctuation). However, when a great deal of the language children encounter in school activities was restricted to items normally found in the oral vocabulary of most six-year-old children (e.g., the Dolch list and the

---

[18] It is important to note that the children who participated in the DISTAR program continued to outperform control children from similar backgrounds. As noted in Adams (1990), they had lower dropout rates, higher percentages of high school graduations, and higher percentages of acceptances to college (Gersten & Keating, 1987).

most common 1000 words), there was little opportunity to expand vocabulary and language skills. *This meant that the main source of language growth continued to be the home (and peers) until well into middle elementary school.* Unfortunately, this also meant that "disadvantaged" children *continued* to have restricted language learning opportunities as their education proceeded.

Becker concluded that disadvantaged children probably needed more direct attention to their language and vocabulary if they were to have a chance at keeping up with their more advantaged peers. I should add that the same is true for children whose first language is not English.

Is there other research to support Becker's contention that disadvantaged children who *can read* show achievement deficits after grade 2? Unfortunately, yes. Jeanne Chall and her colleagues, Vicki Jacobs and Luke Baldwin, similarly found that working class children with strong word identification skills progressively lost ground from second to seventh grade; their vocabulary and reading comprehension scores — above grade level in grades 2 and 3 — were well behind grade level by grade 7. Vocabulary gaps appeared first (in fourth grade), then word recognition (in grade 6), and finally, reading comprehension (noticeably, in grade 7) (Chall, Jacobs, & Baldwin, 1991).

Why were the children in Chall's study "above grade level" (as a group) in grade 2, but below grade level by grade 7? As Becker noted, in grade 2, the vocabulary demands of *reading* comprehension tests are relatively low, largely because most children's skills for identifying words in print are not strong in grade 2. Chall's children had had a good reading program and were somewhat above average in reading skills at the end of grade 2. However, by grade 7 a much larger proportion of children have mastered word identification skills. Variation in the vocabulary and comprehension tests at this grade level reflect differences in the range of words *understood* rather than the range of words that can be *read*. Note, however, that words that can't be read still won't be understood in print.

The Limited Effects of Schooling on Vocabulary Development

Maria Cantalini (1987) found direct evidence that schooling in kindergarten and grades 1 and 2 has no impact on vocabulary growth. Her study of school "readiness" contrasted January- or February-born children (the oldest children in Ontario classrooms) with November- and December-born children (the youngest). In this research design, "young" first-grade children were about the same age as "old" kindergarten children but had an additional year of schooling. The same contrast was made for "young" second-grade children and "old" first-graders.

Cantalini assessed their vocabulary (Peabody Picture Vocabulary Test), and reading and mathematics achievement (WRAT). She found that there was *no* difference between the old kindergarten and young first-graders in vocabulary, nor between the old first-graders and young second-graders. Observed vocabulary differences between the "young" and "old" groups were entirely due to *age*, not school experience. She also found that "young" first-grade children made, on average, *half* the progress in reading as "old" first-grade children. The same was true in grade 2.

This study took place in a mixed rural-urban school district with traditional kindergarten and primary programs. This meant a combination of free or center-based play and a relatively small amount (30–40 minutes) of teacher-directed whole class activities in kindergarten. The primary programs involved traditional basal reading instruction. Like most North American kindergarten and primary programs, the programs Cantalini studied had *no* small-group activities that were primarily concerned with building listening vocabulary and comprehension rather than building reading (word identification) skills.

Frederick Morrison and his colleagues, Megan Williams and Greta Massetti, have reported virtually identical findings for vocabulary in studies conducted in North Carolina (1998). Again, the average vocabularies of "young" first-graders were about the same size as those of "old" kindergarten children at the end of the school year.

Cantalini's and Morrison's findings are not evidence that kindergarten and early elementary programs *can't* help children expand their language. The point is simply that many programs *don't* promote language growth — as both Becker and Chall found. We will look at programs that *do* promote language development in kindergarten and later grades in the next two chapters.

Levels of Language Challenge in the Upper Elementary Grades

Jeanne Chall and Sue Conard (1991) examined levels of vocabulary demand ("readability") in "reading" and "content area" (social studies, science) texts in elementary and high schools. They found vocabulary demands *lower* in "reading texts" than in the content area books. *They also found that well under half of "average" fourth- and sixth-grade students (as determined by a standardized achieve-*

ment test) were able to comprehend "grade level" science and social studies texts. The few "below average" students in their sample were at an even greater disadvantage. In short, the vocabulary "challenge" was above what many students could handle. At the same time, *reading* texts were found to be well below student abilities. Chall and Conard recommended reversing this pattern — challenging and extending students' language in their reading or language arts instruction, while making an effort to ensure that students can understand texts from which they are expected to learn subject content. Although not stated explicitly, it is also clear that students at markedly different levels of reading comprehension will require different texts unless the less advanced students receive substantial vocabulary assistance while reading.

Acquiring Vocabulary "From Context"

Many reading theorists acknowledge that children bring large vocabulary differences to school, and that primary programs do little to redress such differences (e.g., Anderson, 1996; Nagy & Herman, 1987) These theorists argue that with adequate reading skills (word identification), children will be able to acquire larger vocabularies through reading widely. This assumes that children will expand their vocabularies as a result of reading many books — in other words, that children will learn new words "from context."

Is there evidence to support the assumptions that children with limited vocabularies can improve this situation by reading widely, and that they can learn new words "from context" without having definitions supplied? As is often the case in education, the answer is "yes and no." The strongest evidence *for* acquiring large English vocabularies is the successful performance of some children who enter school speaking no English but proceed to do well academically. This is especially true for children who enter an English-speaking school by the beginning of first grade (Wright, Kane, & Deosaran, 1976), and for children whose parents place a high value on educational achievement. However, the available data suggests that many children who enter school from non-English-speaking families continue to lag behind English-speaking children in vocabulary (Biemiller, 1998; Valdes, 1998).

Evidence about adding new vocabulary items. Only a few studies have examined the learning of new lexical items "from context," that is, without formal instruction. One of the earliest was Werner and Kaplan's famous monograph (1952). They would provide a sentence including a pseudoword that represented an unfamiliar concept. For example, "A corplum may be used for support.") They would ask what a child thought *corplum* meant. Then they would supply another sentence ("Corplums may be used to close off an open space,") and so on through five sentences.

Werner and Kaplan carried out this procedure with children in grades 3 to 7. Even after having heard all five sentences, only 7% of third-grade children could arrive at the meaning Werner and Kaplan had intended. By grade 7, less than half did so. (For Werner and Kaplan, "corplum" was a stick or piece of wood.) Clearly, even younger children would have great difficulty acquiring truly *new* words (with new referents) by this means. Elshout-Mohr and van Daalen-Kapteijns (1987) report similar results with college students. Results were especially poor for "less verbally able" college students. New "words" were rarely understood completely, and "low verbal ability" college students were entirely unable to infer correct meanings for them.

Carol Fraser (in press) studied English word acquisition by eight French-speaking college students who were studying English. She had them read a complex passage in economics. They reported using several strategies to cope with unknown words — seeking assistance, consciously trying to infer word meanings, and simply skipping a word. Overall, about a quarter of "new words" (as identified by the students) were retained. Fraser's findings suggest that a combination of inference and checking inferences with an English speaker was most effective (leading to 50% retention), while checking with others or inferring alone were less effective, and of course "ignoring" was ineffective. Bear in mind that these findings refer to college students who were specifically trained to infer words.

William Nagy, Patricia Herman, and Richard Anderson (1985) did find some slight evidence of word learning from context. They had eighth-grade children ("average and above-average readers") read one of two 1000-word passages. Fourteen difficult words were identified for each passage (e.g., *envision, levee*). Students knew about half of these words without reading the passages. After reading a passage, they showed an average gain of about *one* word! They were more likely to acquire words which occurred several times in a passage than those which occurred only once. *Below average* readers, who most need to acquire larger vocabularies, were not included in the study.

Other studies (which will be described in Chapter Four) have indicated somewhat higher rates of vocabulary acquisition from *unassisted* inference. For example, Warwick Elley (1989) reports that an average of three words might be acquired from listening to a story three times during a week. (The Nagy, Herman, and Anderson study provided a single 20-minute period to read a thousand-word passage — allowing for it to be read two or three times, but not requiring that this be done.) Perhaps students can only infer meaning for one unfamiliar word while reading a story or other text. Elley's finding involved three readings. We do not know if more contextual experiences (e.g., reading or listening to thousands of words in a week or several stories) could lead to acquiring more new words.

It should be noted that in the Nagy and Anderson study, there were relatively few difficult words in proportion to the total text. In general, it seems probable that when there are more unfamiliar words in a passage, it becomes harder to learn new words. I assume that "learning from context" implies an understanding of that context. As the proportion of unfamiliar words increases, understanding declines (Freebody & Anderson, 1983; Marks, Doctorow, & Wittrock, 1974). As we have seen, some studies indicate that less "verbally able" students do very poorly at inferring meanings of unknown words (e.g., Elshout-Mohr & van Daalen-Kapteijns, 1987; Robbins & Ehri, 1994; Werner and Kaplan, 1952). This may reflect the consequences of starting with a smaller vocabulary — so that whatever passage is used for "context" contains *more* unfamiliar words for "less able" or lower vocabulary students than for others. Such students may also have some constitutional difficulty which makes word-learning more difficult. It is likely that the two conditions exacerbate each other.

Contextual Vocabulary Acquisition: Evidence from Miscue Studies. Additional evidence on the effect of passage difficulty on student ability to comprehend and to acquire new vocabulary comes from studies of reading "miscues" or oral reading errors. The study of oral reading errors or "miscues" has been a useful way to examine the role of context and meaning in the reading process (Allington, 1984; Biemiller, 1994; Goodman, 1973). A number of studies have consistently shown that children make proportionately fewer "contextual" miscues[19] — errors that reflect attention to the *meaning* of the passage — when their overall error rate is over 4–5% (A. Adams, 1991; Biemiller, 1979, 1994; Blaxall & Willows, 1984) This suggests that when error rates exceed 4–5% of running words, the "understanding" of the text is sufficiently disrupted so that readers are no longer able to use context to facilitate word identification. It seems probable that lack of knowledge of more than 4–5% of running words would

---

[19] "Contextual errors" are errors that are syntactically and semantically consistent with the prior context of the passage being read.

similarly make inferring word meanings unlikely.

Cumulative Vocabulary Deficits. Children who enter third or fourth grade with restricted vocabularies relative to the texts being used will have greater difficulty in comprehending these reading materials and greater difficulty in adding to their vocabulary through reading. This leads to what I call a *cumulative vocabulary deficit* — restricted vocabulary makes it harder to add new vocabulary and probably leads to reduced amounts of reading. Reduced reading in turn continues to restrict vocabulary development. This is what Keith Stanovich (1986) called a "Matthew Effect" in reading — better readers read more and continue to improve both their vocabulary and print skills, while poor readers read less and make little progress.

Summary. I agree with the overall conclusion of Beck & McKeown (1991) that "learning from context does not come easily or in large quantities" (p. 801). They provide a useful summary:

> From the research that has been done, what can be concluded about the role of printed context in accounting for vocabulary growth during the school years? The ubiquitous finding that learning word meanings from context does not seem to occur with particular ease suggests three possible explanations to account for vocabulary growth: One is that learners encounter such a huge number of contextual word-learning opportunities that impressive growth is possible even when the effect of each opportunity is minute. A second explanation is that oral contexts continue to play a major role in vocabulary learning throughout the school years. A third explanation is that vocabulary size and growth have been substantially overestimated. Because available data do not allow selecting with confidence among these three explanations, there seems to be a clear need for research that will clarify the issues. Research is needed that will give some insight into the contribution of oral context to vocabulary growth. Also needed are large-scale studies of vocabulary size that correct for the problems of earlier research in that area. (p. 803)

I will add to their conclusion the general hypothesis that we learn most of our *root* words when we encounter them in context (spoken or print) and *ask* for word meanings — usually asking a teacher or a friend, sometimes "asking" a dictionary. In addition, a number of words are taught by teachers without students asking for them, or are explicitly defined in books. Less frequently, we intentionally infer the meaning of unfamiliar words. I suspect that only rarely do we acquire root word meanings "incidentally" — without conscious effort. (The acquisition of derived word meanings may well occur through context, if there is a learning process required.[20] At present, there seems to be no research examining children's and adolescent's actual word acquisition practices.[21]

Other Sources of Vocabulary Acquisition

"Structural" or Morphological Analysis. Jeremy Anglin's (1993) study of vocabulary development suggests that for about 40–50% of words known by children, there was direct evidence that they worked out meanings by overtly combining prefixes and suffixes (e.g., *un-, -able*) with known root words or by analyzing compound words into their components. In the upper elementary grades, instruction in vocabulary strategies of this type is often referred to as "structural analysis." Children are made aware of the role of prefixes, suffixes, etc. in constructing and determining word meaning. They are typically also taught basic dictionary skills (alphabetizing, using dictionary definitions, using pronunciation guides), though not often given much opportunity to consolidate such skills through extended practice (Durkin, 1979). White, Power, and White (1989) provide an excellent analysis of the power of structural analysis (or "morphological" analysis, as they and Anglin call it). White et al. also provide much information on widely used prefixes and suffixes. Unfortunately, there is no major study directly examining the consequences of extended instruction in using word-learning strategies (Graves, in press). However, in view of Anglin's evidence that children commonly use such word-learning strategies, it seems reasonable to include instruction of these in an effective language program. In Chapter Five, I will describe one successful experimental effort to teach children to use prefixes to identify words. I recommend readers to Graves, Juel, and Graves's (1998) chapter on vocabulary development, and especially the sections on "using word parts" and "using the dictionary."

The Role of Controlled-Vocabulary Readers or "Basals." In some states and provinces, most primary and some upper elementary children read "basal" readers. By definition, a basal reader series adds vocabulary at a planned rate and

---

[20] I suspect that with many derived words (e.g., *unhappy* as opposed to *happy*), there may be no intentional word learning — the word is understood just as a plural or past tense is understood without an elaborate semantic process.

[21] My colleagues and I are presently engaged in research on how children and adolescents learn new words.

level, and ensures frequent use of a word once introduced. In the primary years, this keeps the print word identification load manageable. For older children (grades 3 to 6), this ensures coverage of a specifiable vocabulary. Unfortunately, vocabulary loads are often kept fairly low in basal readers (Chall, 1983; Chall & Conard, 1991; Bond & Dykstra, 1967/1997). Thus while the basal model provides a potential curriculum approach to building vocabulary, in practice the basal method has led to overly low levels of vocabulary being introduced (Chall & Conard, 1991). Worse, the same books are often used with all children, ensuring vocabulary overload for some and lack of challenge for others. No effort is made to assess vocabulary or comprehension levels of children relative to the textbooks being used.

In many other states and provinces, an emphasis on "whole language," "novel study," etc. has led to a de-emphasis or abolition of basal readers, replacing them with "trade books" — books written for children and for parents to read to children, or children's literature. Such books are generally written with less concern for using or introducing a specific vocabulary, and usually do not involve deliberate sequences of increasing vocabulary load. For children with above-average vocabularies and above-average reading (word identification) skills, challenging trade books and novels may well be superior to vocabulary-controlled basal readers because they offer a wide vocabulary and sometimes a higher level of narrative or expository complexity. However, for children with below average vocabulary *or* reading skills, the use of trade books may *reduce* the opportunity to build vocabulary and language skills.

For example, a study of the effects of "whole language" instruction on third-graders in a Canadian school district found an overrepresentation of children performing *below* the 25th percentile on standardized tests (Glasspool & Hutton, 1993). The same study also showed an overrepresentation of children *above* the 75th percentile, suggesting that for those whose reading (word identification skills) and vocabulary levels were *high*, the shift to trade books was advantageous.

An important issue centers around the relative effectiveness of using basals which deliberately introduce and repeat new vocabulary, versus the currently-popular approach of having children repeatedly reading the same story as a means of building vocabulary and comprehension. We will revisit this issue in the next chapter.

Conclusion

Schools now provide little or no alternative language support in the primary years to compensate for differences in experience before age five. In the upper elementary years, some direct language and vocabulary instruction is provided, but the rapidly increasing language demands of texts are greater than many students can handle successfully.

When we allow children to arrive at third or fourth grade unprepared for the vocabulary and other language demands of post-primary schooling, we reduce their chances for further educational progress even if they have become effective "readers" at the level of identifying words in print. For children who arrive at fourth grade with significantly below-average vocabularies and language skills, understanding "fourth grade texts" is rather like trying to climb a cliff at the base of a hill. If one has the requisite language, one is already at the top of the cliff and can continue to go up the educational hill. But those missing the necessary language (mostly vocabulary) are at the bottom of the cliff. They try to scramble up while others continue to extend their knowledge.

Schooling cannot "compensate" for *all* constitutional and experiential differences. But surely we can do better than the zero school effect on vocabulary growth observed in two studies described here. There is evidence that language can be substantially affected by experiences in which children are exposed to a wider range of meaningful vocabulary and the meanings of unfamiliar words are explained. In the next two chapters, we will look at some of this evidence that teachers *can* have a major impact on language development and comprehension. Chapter Four examines what can be done in the primary years, when fostering comprehension means fostering listening comprehension. In Chapter Five, we will consider ways of facilitating comprehension in the upper elementary years, involving language which is read as well as language which is heard.

Chapter Four

Promoting Language In Kindergarten and the Primary Grades

Thus far, I have been demonstrating the necessity of providing a greater emphasis on building listening comprehension and oral language in the elementary curriculum. We have seen:

- That oral language development sets a limit on reading comprehension.
- That children arrive at school (kindergarten) with widely varying levels of oral language comprehension.
- That current educational practice has little impact on oral language development in the primary years.
- That children who enter grade 4 with lagging vocabulary will come to lag in reading comprehension even if their reading (word identification skills) are strong. Poor vocabulary at this point leads to growing gaps in reading comprehension even though more attention is paid to vocabulary issues in the upper elementary grades.
- While increased attention to vocabulary and language development is not going to eliminate age and experience differences, such attention can probably "narrow the gap" between high and low achieving children by increasing opportunities for average and especially low vocabulary children to encounter and learn a wider range of vocabulary.

There is clear evidence that environmental factors play a role in the early development of language. As summarized in Chapter Two, both observational and experimental studies have shown that the amount and quality of adult talk with children is highly correlated with language outcomes. Many of these studies involve data on mothers and their children, and it could be argued that the observed relationship between child language and maternal talk with children is simply a consequence of genetic endowment passed from mother to child.

However, the experimental studies of Tizard and Whitehurst and their colleagues (see Chapter Two) clearly demonstrate that increased exposure to language and better adult-child interaction really results in improved child language. Furthermore, both of these groups of experimental studies demonstrated rates of vocabulary acquisition well above "average rates" as determined by standardized test norms. In short, there are things we can do to help children build language. Thus there is both observational and experimental evidence that language and especially vocabulary development can be considerably enhanced. Let us turn now to ways of promoting language development in kindergarten and the early primary grades.

Illustrative Preschool/Kindergarten Studies

In this section, I will describe several studies which demonstrated significant impacts on vocabulary for children in preschool or kindergarten programs.

A naturalistic study showing the power of teachers to influence vocabulary. In an important study of the impact of different teacher approaches to reading, David Dickinson and Miriam Smith (1994) reported that much of the variation in vocabulary in different groups of Head Start children[22] could be predicted by knowing about how their teachers went about reading to them. Dickinson and Smith also reported that children whose teachers who primarily dialogued with students *before* and *after reading,* but not much *during* reading, had the greatest vocabulary gains. I suspect that these effective teachers did address vocabulary problems while reading, but did not *unnecessarily* interrupt the flow of the stories they were reading. Furthermore, there is evidence that children won't pick up more than two or three words per session.[23] More generally, Dickinson and Smith's work demonstrates that what teachers *do* makes a difference; in the case of language, some ways of teaching lead to significantly greater vocabulary growth than others.

Grover Whitehurst: Dialogic Reading (urban middle-class and disadvantaged children). Grover Whitehurst and his colleagues have been developing a program

---

[22] Technically, "variance" is a measure of how much individual cases differ from the average. In this case, "accounting for a percentage of variance" means showing that the variation in individual classes is considerably less than the variation of children combined across classes.

[23] The effects of more than one language challenge or vocabulary building experience per day have not been tested.

for fostering language through "reading" to children called "Dialogic Reading." Whitehurst et al. (1994) describe this program:

> Dialogic reading differs substantially from the manner that adults typically read picture books to children. A shift of roles is central: In typical book reading, the adult reads and the child listens, but in dialogic reading, the child learns to become the storyteller. The adult then assumes the role of an active listener, asking questions, adding information, and prompting the child to increase the sophistication of his or her description of the material in the picture book. As the child becomes more skillful in the role of story teller, the adult is encouraged to ask open-ended questions and avoid yes/no or pointing questions. For example, the adult might say, "What is Eeyore doing?" or "You tell me about this page" instead of "Is Eeyore lying down?" (p. 680)[24]

Several different studies have been carried out. Whitehurst, Falco, et al. (1988) demonstrated that middle-class mothers using Dialogic Reading with their two-year-old children produced eight-month language gains in six weeks of daily 20–30-minute reading sessions. A control group who spent as much time just reading to their children showed normal gains (i.e., six weeks' worth) over the same period. Arnold et al. (1994) replicated these findings and showed that adults could be successfully taught dialogic reading methods by videotape. In this study, middle-class children aged two and a half years whose mothers used Dialogic Reading for four weeks had average gains of 3.3 months on the Peabody Vocabulary Test compared with children whose mothers simply read to them.

These studies demonstrate that children's environments do affect their language growth. However, they involved one-to-one reading — a level of support not possible in typical school settings. Furthermore, both studies involved advantaged children. In another study, Whitehurst et al. (1994) used a day care setting for disadvantaged children, in which caregivers read to groups of 5 four-year-old children at a time. Some groups of children were also read to at home. Both the caregivers and the parents were trained in Dialogic Reading using the videotapes reported in Arnold et al. (1994). A six-week interval of daily 10-minute Dialogic Reading sessions lead to a gain of only 2.5 words from the material read, and gains of about 0.5 months on standardized vocabulary tests, compared with control children who did not participate in Dialogic Reading.

---

[24] Manuals, demonstration videotapes can be purchased from Dr. Whitehurst at the Department of Psychology, State University of New York at Stony Brook, Stony Brook, NY.

These group effects are considerably less impressive than the parent-to-child results. Still, if these gains could be sustained over a year, Dialogic Reading could lead to a six-month vocabulary gain on the Peabody compared with no intervention.

Dina Feitelson and colleagues: Daily Story Reading with Definitions (disadvantaged Arab children in Israel). In a more extended study with kindergarten children, Dina Feitelson and her colleagues (1991) arranged for twelve books to be read to Arabic-speaking children over a five-month period. The books explicitly used a formal version of Arabic (FusHa) commonly used in print but not in colloquial speech. One book was read to the whole class for about twenty minutes at the end of each school day. Each book was read about nine times over the course of five months. Prior to each reading session, the teachers explained up to three unfamiliar words. While reading, teachers sometimes also noted colloquial equivalents of words used in the text.

On a test of listening comprehension (not involving content from the 12 stories), children who had been read to were near the maximum possible score (averaging 6 correct out of 7 items), while those who had not been read to regularly, but had had language lessons, averaged 3.7 out of 7 items. Significant gains were also reported on other measures of language performance. Unfortunately, Feitelson et al. did not report any specific data on vocabulary. These results underestimate the effect of the program; many children could presumably have scored higher on a more advanced test. Moreover, Feitelson reports that the children were asking for new stories. More stories could probably have been introduced.

Especially noteworthy is the fact that the children were not only acquiring the vocabulary and knowledge of story structure needed to comprehend this material, but also the more formal dialect of Arabic used in most written communications. In disadvantaged English-speaking communities, there is also a need to acquire standard forms of the language used in "educated" contexts.

Feitelson reports similar results for eight classes of Hebrew-speaking kindergarten children. Feitelson, Kita, and Goldstein (1986) also carried out a reading-experience study with first-graders which will be discussed in the next section.

Kindergarten Studies: Conclusion. Thus we have examples of small vocabulary gains with preschoolers despite six weeks of small-group "instruction," but large gains with kindergartners who were read to daily for five months *and who were given definitions and clarifications when needed* — at a whole-class level. What makes the difference? Is it age? The volume of experience and number of repetitions in Feitelson's study? Would Feitelson's methods have worked with groups of younger children? It is clear that we need to provide some definition or clarification of unfamiliar words. This happened both in Whitehurst's study and Feitelson's. When no supporting definition or clarification of new words is given, as in a kindergarten study by Robbins and Ehri (1994), gains are weak. As noted in the previous chapter, depending on children to extract meanings from context appears to be a very inefficient way of building vocabulary — especially *root* word vocabulary.

Illustrative Grade 1 and 2 Studies

Dina Feitelson and colleagues: Daily Story Reading with Definitions (disadvantaged, Hebrew-speaking children in grade 1). As with the kindergarten studies described above, the teacher read to the whole class for about 20 minutes at the end of the school day over a six month period (Feitelson, Keitel, & Goldstein, 1986). "Hard words" were clarified as needed. Fifteen books were read from a series about "Kofiko," a mischievous monkey who sounds rather like "Curious George." Although disapproved of by teachers, these books were extremely popular with the children, many of whom insisted that their parents get copies of some of the books. Although initially three classrooms were involved in the reading intervention, two dropped out because the teachers were unwilling to give up time from their short teaching day (3.5 hours) for daily oral reading to their students.

Children in the remaining experimental class were contrasted with children from two control classes. All came from the same neighborhood, but those in the control classes scored significantly higher on a vocabulary test (the Israeli version of WISC) prior to the reading intervention. Unfortunately, this vocabulary test was not re-administered at the end of the study. Despite this difference, by the end of the study the children who had been read to daily showed higher achievement in comprehension of a reading passage (82% vs. 63% accurate), in oral reading of a "technical" passage (94% vs. 79% accurate), and used longer sentences when asked to tell a story (5.6 versus 4.5 words per sentence). While a study involving only one experimental classroom is limited,[25] I have included this study because it suggests that time invested in listen-

---

[25] The differences could always have been due to qualities of the one teacher or other factors.

ing to stories (with clarifications as needed) is time well spent, even when the time available for instruction is perceived to be very short.[26]

Warwick Elley: Inferring Words from One Story, With or Without Clarifications of Word Meanings *(urban and suburban children in first and second grade in New Zealand).* In the first study, grade 1 teachers read a story (*Gumdrop at Sea*) to their class without any explanation of words (Elley, 1989). The story took approximately 10 minutes to read and contained 20 words thought to be unfamiliar. Children's knowledge of these words was pretested a week before the story was read. At this time, the children knew on average 9 of the 20 words (multiple choice test). A week later, the story was read three times, separated by 3- or 4-day intervals. No explanation of words was given, nor was there any discussion of the story. Overall, the children now knew over 12 of the 20 words, or a gain of 3 words over a week with 3 readings of the same story. The children differed markedly in how many words they knew initially — ranging from 66% in the highest-scoring quarter of the children to 26% in the lowest-scoring quarter. However, gains were similar for all of these ability groups at about 3 words — except for the lowest group, which gained 4 words over a week of reading.

In a second study, Elley contrasted acquisition of words with no accompanying explanation versus acquisition when words were explained as they occurred in context (Elley, 1989). In this study, done with grade 2 children, the stories used were *Rapscallion Jones* (Marshall, 1983) and *The White Crane* (trans. Smith, 1983). Again, approximately 20 low-familiarity words were included in each story. Results showed both the importance of explanation and the importance of choice of stories. For *Rapscallion Jones*, explanations improved vocabulary acquisition over three readings from 3 words without explanations to 8 words with explanations. Again, children who initially knew more words added fewer words than those who initially knew fewer words. Words in *The White Crane* proved much harder to acquire. Without explanations, children acquired an average of 1 word after hearing the story three times. With explanations of words, they acquired 3 words. Overall, the power of simple vocabulary explanations during story reading to facilitate vocabulary learning from context was impressive.

It is not known why there was less learning with *The White Crane*, although

---

26 Actually, because they taught for six days a week, the Israeli teachers had nearly the same classroom time — 21 hours — as many North American teachers have once recess, gym, etc. are removed.

teachers reported "less involvement" with the story. The context was Japan in winter, so perhaps children in New Zealand have little experience with either winter or Japan. Elley also notes that there was little action and no humor in the story. Robbins and Ehri (1994) also reported considerable variation in words learned in two different stories. In that study, some children learned about three words from story reading without explanations, but there was a similar difference between numbers of words learned in different stories.

Both the Feitelson and Elley studies are remarkable for the magnitude of language gains produced from relatively short daily *whole class* interventions. In Elley's best case, 3 sessions totaling 40 minutes of reading with vocabulary explanation led to an average gain of 8 words in a week. There was evidence that most of these words were still known three months later. The Feitelson study provides no basis for directly estimating vocabulary gains. However, the dramatic increase in listening comprehension clearly indicates vocabulary and other language gains.

Anne Brown and Annemarie Palincsar: Reciprocal Teaching (urban first-grade "high risk" children whose poor initial progress led to their placement on waiting lists for special education). Palincsar and Brown's (1984) "reciprocal teaching" is a complex teaching approach intended to increase children's reading comprehension. Initially developed for children around sixth grade, Brown and Palincsar (1989) have adapted the program for facilitating listening comprehension in first grade. They describe reciprocal teaching as follows:

> Reciprocal teaching takes place in a cooperative learning group that features guided practice in applying simple concrete strategies to the task of text comprehension. The basic procedure is simple. An adult teacher and a group of students take turns leading a discussion on the contents of a section of text that they are jointly attempting to understand. *[Note: Texts used are usually expository. AB]* The discussions are free ranging, but four strategic activities must be practiced routinely: *questioning, clarifying, summarizing,* and *predicting. [In examples given by Brown and Palincsar, "clarifying" frequently amounts to defining or explaining words in context. AB]* The dialogue leader begins the discussion by asking a question on the main content and ends by summarizing the gist. If there is disagreement, the group rereads and discusses potential candidates for question and summary statements until they reach consensus. Summarizing provides a means by which the group can monitor its progress, noting points of agreement and disagreement. Particularly valuable is the fact that summarizing at the end of a period of discus-

sion helps students establish where they are in preparation for tackling a new segment of text. Attempts to clarify any comprehension problems that might arise are also an integral part of the discussions. And finally, the leader asks for predictions about future content. Throughout, the adult teacher provides guidance and feedback tailored to the needs of the current discussion leader and his or her respondents. (Brown & Palincsar, 1989, p. 413)

In adapting the program for first graders, the teacher read the text. Twenty sessions were carried out with groups of six children (four "at risk" and two others). With some training, the children began to assume the discussion leader role, providing questions and summaries. Improvements in comprehension were assessed by reading other texts to intervention group children and control group children and asking questions about these. At the beginning of the program, about 50% of these questions were answered correctly. Over time, the control group showed no change. However, after 10 sessions, the reciprocal teaching children were about 60% accurate, and by the end of the 20 sessions, they were over 70% accurate. About 75% of the children made gains. As with the Feitelson study, we do not have explicit vocabulary data, but we do have evidence of improved language comprehension.

Reciprocal teaching is an elaborate small-group mode of instruction which requires considerable teacher preparation (Brown & Campione, 1994). It goes well beyond simply trying to expand vocabulary and language proficiency to generally trying to foster increased self-direction and knowledge building in the context of carefully planned curricula. Can we learn practices from this work that can be applied to the simpler goal of fostering listening comprehension? Are complex and elaborate approaches necessary for successful language growth?

Two features of reciprocal teaching deserve special attention. First, we see again that providing *clarification* of words appears to be a necessary component of language building. It can happen in whole classes (Feitelson, Elley), small groups (Whitehurst, Brown & Campione), or individuals (Whitehurst, Wells). However, with any of these group structures, clarification — explaining what unfamiliar words mean — is a necessary component of successful language teaching. This sounds patently obvious. Unfortunately, we have seen much evidence that too little clarification goes on in many school programs — for example, the finding that children do not learn vocabulary at school, and Durkin's (1978) evidence that little comprehension/vocabulary instruction actually occurs in most classrooms.

A second feature of Brown and Palincsar's and Whitehurst's work is the emphasis on students taking active roles in language activities. If children are to *use* language to describe and regulate their world, they must do more than respond to teacher questions — they must initiate verbal descriptions and accounts on their own. For example, in reciprocal teaching, students take turns assuming responsibility for leading discussion groups. We will return to this issue in Chapter Five.

Rachel Brown, Michael Pressley and colleagues: Transactional Strategies Instruction (disadvantaged second-graders).[27] Transactional Strategies Instruction (TSI) is another complex teaching approach intended to increase children's reading or language comprehension, specifically, "use of strategic processing whenever students encounter demanding text" (Brown et al., 1996, p. 19). This is a complete approach to literacy instruction which is meant to be applied over several years, not a brief "intervention." The authors use the term *strategic processing* to refer to a number of specific strategies that can be invoked to guide problem-solving when one experiences a failure of comprehension. Examples include relating current texts to prior knowledge, seeking clarification when meaning is obscure, visualizing events being read, summarizing content periodically, and generating questions and interpretations while reading. There is also focus on effective word recognition strategies. As such, there are many parallels to reciprocal teaching. Specific instructional methods include direct teaching of "strategies," guidance in the use of strategies as students read and discuss texts, emphasis on *when* particular strategies would be useful, discussion of text content, emphasis on using the same approaches when reading subject content (e.g., social studies, math texts), and emphasis on the value of learning. An example of a strategy is "visualization" — constructing a mental picture of an event described in a text. Much more detail is provided in Pressley et al., 1992; and Brown et al., 1996.

In a recent full-year trial with second-graders, Brown et al. (1996) found gains of 19% on reading comprehension across 5 groups of disadvantaged children compared with 5 groups of matched children who received conventional instruction. Gains in *comprehension* at this level are hard to come by — such gains were not reported in recent studies of other innovative primary curricula — e.g., Reading Recovery and Success for All. I believe this study again

---

[27] This section adapted from Meichenbaum and Biemiller (1998), pp. 234-239, with permission of the authors and publisher.

illustrates the importance in primary reading programs of focus on language in addition to identification of words in print.

Lesley Mandel Morrow: Literature-Based Program (disadvantaged second-graders). This program involved reading to children daily, and three to five 30-minute independent reading and writing periods, in addition to traditional basal reader instruction. Book reading included some introductory questions, clarification of unfamiliar words, and discussion after the story. On average, about 4 hours a week were devoted to language activities and an additional 3.5 hours a week were spent with basals. Comparison children received 7.5 hours a week of basal reader instruction. (Much more detail is available in Morrow, 1992.)

After a year of instruction, the net result was that the children receiving language instruction showed a 50% improvement in *listening* comprehension, while no change was observed in the control group. This is consistent with research reported earlier suggesting that the normal primary curriculum does little to enhance language development. Unfortunately, the program had no impact on common measures of reading comprehension or word identification, probably because nothing was done differently with respect to basic word identification skills. It seems likely that combining this program with something like Becker's DISTAR program would have produced significant gains in reading comprehension as well as listening comprehension.

Conclusion. On the whole, the evidence suggests that whole group story reading with definitions or "clarifications" may be as effective as more elaborate small group interactive programs for promoting *vocabulary* development. To what extent more intense discussion-focused activities, scaffolded to ensure active participation by all members, are necessary to promote *comprehension* development is unclear. We lack contrasts of such programs to simpler, vocabulary-focused approaches.

Chapter Five

Promoting Language in the Upper Elementary Grades

With young children, the keys to expanding language are:

- Engaging the children in stories or other texts which include some new words;
- Providing "clarification" or definitions of unfamiliar words occurring in this language; and *sometimes*
- Creating situations in which children actively talk, using newly acquired language to discuss/describe things they care about. (The evidence is less clear for this point than for the preceding two points.)

To a considerable extent, similar principles apply in work with older children.

I have already referred to Chall, Jacobs, and Baldwin's (1990) book, *The Reading Crisis*, which describes the problems of children entering fourth and higher grades with restricted vocabularies. In this naturalistic study, Chall and her colleagues also found that children showed larger vocabulary and comprehension gains in classrooms where teachers used "challenging" texts (e.g., texts at about *one* readability grade level above the child's *actual reading level*) and used a range of materials in addition to a basal reader.[28] Comprehension gains were also increased by explicit comprehension instruction, library visits, and generally more program time devoted to reading instruction. Not surprisingly, when teachers spend more time on new vocabulary more is learned! As with the Dickinson and Smith (1994) study of kindergarten classrooms, part of the significance of this study is simply demonstrating that *what teachers "do" makes a difference* — that *teachers who provide greater opportunity to learn challenging new words and more instruction about understanding language have students who learn more vocabulary and become more effective users of language.*

---

[28] The effects of a *range* of materials may partly reflect the excessively restricted vocabulary of many basal reading series (Chall & Conard, 1991).

Reviews of Language and Vocabulary-Enhancing Programs

There are two general approaches to fostering language and vocabulary. The simpler, more *instructionally-oriented approach* involves directly teaching vocabulary and vocabulary strategies (e.g., the roles of prefixes, suffixes, word families, etc.), often in conjunction with the use of readings or language material that has been deliberately selected at least in part because of its vocabulary content. The other, more *interactive* and *scaffolded approach* lays greater stress on creating tasks which enhance the autonomy of the learner, while posing problems that will engage the learner in understanding challenging problems and language.[29] This is a continuation of approaches like those of Whitehurst et al. (1994), A. Brown and Palincsar (1989), R. Brown and Pressley (1996), and Morrow (1992) as described in the previous chapter.

Steve Stahl and Marilyn Fairbanks (1986) summarized research on explicit methods of teaching or promoting vocabulary growth. All but two of these studies involved fourth grade or older children. The general conclusion was that "vocabulary instruction" has a very strong effect — especially on words taught, but also on general (untaught) vocabulary. Programs which *combine* direct explanation of words with reading or using the words in context are the most effective. Not surprisingly, lots of experience with target words worked better than one or two exposures. This means either using material in which vocabulary to be learned is deliberately repeated as in basals or subject textbooks, or extensively rereading books — a practice which may prove unpopular with older elementary children.[30] Readers are referred to Stahl's (1998) book *Vocabulary Development,* Volume 2 in this series.

Linda Kucan and Isabel Beck (1997) summarized research on more elabo-

---

[29] *Scaffolding* is a term describing an approach to teaching that goes beyond direct instruction to include an emphasis increasing the student's responsibility for using skills and application strategies independently. There are extended discussions of scaffolding issues and strategies in Stone (1998) — part of a special issue of the *Journal of Learning Disabilities* devoted to scaffolding — and Meichenbaum and Biemiller's *Nurturing Independent Learners* (1998), especially chapters 8-10.

[30] A note on rereading the same story or material: Very young children are notorious for wanting stories read many, many times. They probably need this repetition for any comprehension of extended narrative. Indeed, they may just be focusing on particular words or sentences. By second or third grade, my personal observation is that children do not want most stories or videos more than one or two times, and certainly not repeated on subsequent days. I believe that a really interesting and fruitful line of research would be to assess children's preferences for repeated readings of the same story, and the effects of repeated story reading across the primary age range and at all levels of ability.

rate methods of promoting comprehension through inquiry, instruction, and social interaction. Kucan and Beck note that having students "think aloud" while trying to understand or comprehend text was first done as a research method for studying comprehension. Later, researchers tried teaching students specific verbal "strategies" which had been observed to be used by high-achieving students. (Examples of such strategies are self-directed questions such as "First, I am going to decide if this story has any problems?" as used in Miller, 1985.) In time, some researchers came to question whether the specific "strategies" (e.g., specific self-directed questions) were what mattered, or whether the process of dialoguing with others about text was key (e.g., Rosenshine & Meister, 1994, in a review of reciprocal teaching). This line of research and educational intervention has yielded one substantial finding plus several questions. It is clear that successful comprehension involves not only a passive "attending" to the content of text (whether heard or read), but a kind of active processing initiated by the reader. This can be a monologue by the reader about what the writer means, or a dialogue between two or more readers about what is read. (The same applies to listening.) When this kind of active processing is absent, comprehension is reduced, especially for relatively difficult texts. To foster this kind of dialogue, programs such as Reciprocal Teaching deliberately structure situations in which children *lead* discussions about what they hear or read. The expectation is that discussing texts with others will lead ultimately to the kind of internal dialogue reported by high-achieving readers. Thus children who are used to asking others "summarize this paragraph," are expected to begin asking *themselves* to do so.

Kucan and Beck stress that it is less clear what this finding implies for practical teaching. When is direct instruction and teacher modelling called for? To what extent should specific *strategies* be taught (e.g., Palincsar and Brown's questioning, clarifying, summarizing, and predicting), versus simply having the children dialogue about the text.? To what extent can comprehension be enhanced by promoting discussion among peers or led by teachers? All of these practices have been shown to have a positive impact on comprehension. It is probably the case that each approach is beneficial in the right circumstances, depending on the relative difficulty of text for students (both in terms of word identification demands and comprehension demands), their prior experience with self-directed and collaborative educational tasks, and the ultimate educational objective (e.g., comprehension test performance, increased self-selected reading, long-term educational achievement).

Illustrative Approaches to Promoting Language in the Upper Elementary Grades

Let us turn to some specific studies of classroom methods of achieving language gains.

Michal Shany and Andrew Biemiller: Assisted Reading (urban disadvantaged third- and fourth-graders). The main purpose of this study was to demonstrate the effects of extensive reading practice (Shany & Biemiller, 1995). An unexpected benefit was an increase in listening comprehension for children in one practice condition in which children read while listening to the same text on tape.

Briefly, children in grades 3 or 4, who were initially reading at a mid-first-grade level, read for half an hour a day for 64 sessions (16 weeks). The reading material used was simply old basal readers (Nelson readers, and Dent readers from the 1960s). These were selected to provide effective vocabulary control and systematic addition of new reading vocabulary. Each child read at her or his own pace, and individual assistance was provided for words the children couldn't identify in print. Assistance with *word meanings* was available but rarely requested. There were two "assistance" conditions. In one, the student could turn to a helper who would read any word needed. In the other, the story being read was also provided on tape whose speed the student could adjust to a rate at which she could read the text while listening to it.[31]

Compared to non-treatment children, both assisted groups made similar substantial gains in oral reading speed and accuracy (two grade levels) and reading comprehension (one grade level). In addition, those in the tape-assisted condition made significant gains in listening comprehension — probably as a result of reading more advanced or "challenging" material. During the 16 weeks of the project, both assisted groups read all the way through *two* series of first-, second-, and third-grade basals. Seven of the 10 children in the tape-assisted condition were well into a fourth-grade basal. The tape-assisted group showed a 40% gain in listening comprehension compared to 26% for the control group and 29% for the teacher-assisted group. The tape-assisted group also showed a non-significant gain of 11% on the Peabody Vocabulary Test compared to 6% for the control group and 4% for the teacher-assisted group. The researchers suspect that, had they used just one series of basals and moved into the more

---

[31] It is essential that the tape speed be slightly slower than the child's oral reading rate for that passage. Otherwise, it is impossible for the child to read along while listening.

challenging material sooner, more children might have shown greater listening gains. At any rate, this study demonstrates that simple exposure to new vocabulary with considerable repetition of that vocabulary, as occurs in basal readers, was sufficient to increase listening comprehension and probably vocabulary. This finding is consistent with Chall's observation that added "challenge" (more demanding texts) led to increased vocabulary acquisition and improved comprehension. Another key point is that as little as 30 minutes a day (4 days a week) of reading experience was sufficient to bring about substantial gains in reading and language achievement.

Isabel Beck, Charles Perfetti, and Margaret McKeown: Teaching Words and Promoting "Word Awareness" (urban disadvantaged fourth-graders). This project had a dual purpose. One was to teach the meanings of 104 difficult words including many from the basal reader series (Ginn) that the students would be using. Other words were drawn from similar categories (e.g., "people") as the Ginn words. The other "... expectation of the study was that deep and fluent expertise on a large but limited set of words might arouse a general 'word awareness', leading children to be more cognizant of words in speech and print around them. This in turn might motivate children to use their environment to learn more words." (Beck, Perfetti, & McKeown, 1982)

The program involved 75 daily sessions (18 weeks) of 30 minutes each, running from October to March. Twelve "categories" of 8 words each were introduced over one-week periods. The categories included:

- People,
- Eating,
- Eyes,
- Moods,
- Speaking,
- Ears,
- What you can do with your arms,
- How we move our legs,
- What people can be like,
- More people,
- Working together or apart, and
- The usual and the unusual.

For example, the category *people* included the words: *accomplice, virtuoso, rival, miser, philanthropist, novice, hermit,* and *tyrant.*. Over a five-day period, students would:

- (Day 1) be introduced to the words and their definitions, relate them to associated words (e.g., *clue: accomplice*), and evaluate them (e.g., "yay" or "boo" to *miser?*)

- (Day 2) generate sentences for each word, and play a team game in which words were to be quickly matched to their definition.
- (Day 3) select task contexts for the week's words (e.g., "Would an *accomplice* be more likely to (a) squeal to the police... (b) rob a bank by himself? (c) enjoy babysitting?") and justify their choices. Then they were asked to think of something else these different kinds of "people" might do.
- (Day 4) practice rapid, timed matching of words and definitions, and relate meanings of different words in the category (e.g., "Could an *accomplice* be a *novice*?").
- (Day 5) complete a multiple choice test of the words studied.

Review weeks occurred approximately every third week. Thus there were twelve instructional weeks and six review weeks. Similar games and activities were used. Forty-three of the 104 words received review.

Overall, the program lead to marked gains in general vocabulary and reading comprehension achievement (from the 35th to 45th percentiles). Prior to training, both program and non-program children were at near-chance performance on a 4-alternative multiple choice test of the 104 vocabulary words (30%). Following the 18-week program, students in the program averaged 84% on the taught and reviewed words, and 78% on the taught-only words. The control children were still near chance (34%). Adjusting for guesses on the multiple choice test, the program children acquired an average of 53 of the 104 words (about 4.4 words per week, not counting review weeks), while the non-program children acquired much less than one word per week. Gains were only slightly larger for the words which were practiced twice as much. It could be argued that introducing more new words would be a more effective use of time. We should emphasize the evidence that the program led to general gains in vocabulary as well as specific words learned.

Although this program did not emphasize contextual reading or listening to the target words, many of the words came from the basal series that was being used in the classroom. No data was presented that contrasted the learning of words included in the basal with those not included.

A key practical issue is the choice of words. In this study, many of the words studied are not commonly known until children are considerably beyond fourth grade (e.g., *virtuoso, philanthropist*). Clearly, studying such words yielded effective results. Would a greater emphasis on studying words known by the majority of children at the sixth- to eighth-grade levels have been more useful? We don't know.

Unfortunately, no specific measure of "word awareness" was attempted. However, the large and significant increases on the standardized vocabulary and reading comprehension tests, and an increase of 6 words (14%) on a list of 43 untaught words of similar length and grammatical category indicate some increased attention to vocabulary as a result of the program. Overall, any program that can increase average academic achievement from the 35th to 45th percentiles over 18 weeks is doing something right!

Janet Nicol, Michael Graves, and Wayne Slater: Building Vocabulary through Prefix Instruction (fourth- to sixth grade middle-class children). This was a much less ambitious project, concerned simply with the effects of teaching children to interpret common prefixes (Nicol, Graves, & Slater, 1984). I include it because it illustrates both the ease with which strategies for understanding derived words can be taught, and the degree of vocabulary improvement possible with such instruction. Nicol, Graves, and Slater note that nearly a quarter of the 20,000 commonly-used words on Thorndike's 1932 list contain prefixes. Thus, knowledge of how to interpret the meaning of these prefixes could expand one's vocabulary by up to 33% of the remaining 15,000 words.

The experimental program involved just three half-hour sessions occurring on three consecutive days. The prefixes *re-, in-, de-, sub-, inter-, com-, trans-,* and *en-* were taught. Each prefix was introduced and illustrated in sentences with two common words using the prefix and two less common words. For example, the prefix *re-* was introduced as meaning "again." A common *re-* word was "*rewrite.*" A less common *re-* word was "refortify." Here are illustrative sentences from Nicol et al.:

- Tom was asked to *rewrite* the paper because it was too messy.
  rewrite — to write again.
- After some of the castle walls were battered by enemy cannon fire, the soldiers rushed to *refortify* their stronghold.
  refortify — to make strong again.

Each prefix was introduced with sentences like those above. A number of written exercises provided practice in interpreting words with each prefix. These were self-corrected immediately after they were done. On the first day, a total of three prefixes were introduced in this manner. Three more were introduced on the second day, and the final two on the third day, along with a review of all eight prefixes.

This was done in one fourth-, one fifth-, and one sixth-grade classroom. Comparable classrooms served as non-instructed controls. Prior to instruction, all of the children knew about 30% of the words to be covered in the instruction. Three weeds afterwards, the instructed group knew 85% of the words, while the uninstructed group knew 35% of them. On a set of transfer words (using the prefixes but not included in the lessons), both groups knew about 53% prior to instruction. After instruction, the group taught prefixes correctly interpreted 84%, while the uninstructed group was now 58% correct. Although details are not given, Nicol et al. report positive effects at all three grades, and with lower- as well as higher-achieving students. Clearly, prefix instruction was highly successful. Clearly, many prefixed words were not known prior to instruction. We don't know if the root words to which prefixes applied were also not known. However, since there was a marked gain on uninstructed words for the instructed group, we can infer that in many cases they knew enough about the root words to successfully apply the prefixes.

Nicol et al. note that there are approximately 20 common prefixes, and recommend teaching all of them across the upper elementary grades.

Ann Brown and Joseph Campione: Fostering Communities of Learners *(disadvantaged fourth- to sixth-graders).*[32] As with several programs described earlier in this book, the overall objective of the "Communities of Learners" program is to improve active comprehension of language. Brown and Campione (1996) summarize this as

> ... critical thinking and reflection skills underlying multiple forms of higher literacy: reading, writing, argumentation, technological sophistication, and so forth. Although billed as a thinking curriculum, the FCL program is embedded in deep disciplinary content *[e.g., it involves learning basic concepts in a discipline, in this case, biology. AB]*. One cannot think critically, or otherwise, in a vacuum. Food for thought is needed to nourish critical thinking and reflection (p. 290).

To achieve these broad aims, they engage students in the study of a particular area or topic, e.g., endangered species, or giant cockroaches. Students participate in a number of different learning settings or "participation structures." Some of these settings are designed to foster *acquiring knowledge* through reading, lectures, Internet sources, etc. Other settings are intended to foster *consult-*

---

[32] This description is adapted from Meichenbaum and Biemiller (1998), pp. 250-256, with permission of the authors and publisher.

ing about that knowledge by working with fellow students to teach what was learned to others. Brown and Campione summarize the program as follows:

> At its simplest level, there are three key parts. Students engage in independent and group research on some aspect of a topic of inquiry, mastery of which is ultimately the responsibility of all members of the class. This requires that they share their expertise with their classmates. This sharing is further motivated by some consequential task or activity that demands that all students have learned about all aspects of the joint topic. This consequential task can be as traditional as a test or quiz, or some nontraditional activity such as designing a "biopark" to protect an endangered species. These three key activities — (a) research, (b) in order to share information, (c) in order to perform a consequential task — are all overseen and coordinated by (d) self-conscious reflection on the part of all members of the community. In addition, the research-share-perform cycles of FCL cannot be carried out in a vacuum. All rely on the fact that the participants are trying to understand deep disciplinary content (Brown & Campione, 1996, pp. 292-293)

In studies of the FCL program, a variety of assessments have been provided, ranging from fairly traditional reading comprehension tests to analyses of changes in argumentation and explanation (Brown & Campione, 1994). In comparison with (presumably similar) non-FCL sixth-grade children, the FCL children (1) showed large gains in reading comprehension (65% versus 25% correct on a reading comprehension test that did not involve material covered in the FCL classes); (2) applied more biological principles (e.g., "animals need and find shelter") in constructing an imaginary animal (6 vs. 1 — both groups had studied biology during the term); and (3) could answer many more short-answer questions concerning topics studied in the FCL classes, but only read about in the non-FCL classes. Overall, in early trials, the program appears to be succeeding at improving students' abilities to comprehend texts. The authors stress that some of this improvement will necessarily be "local" — related to areas of new student expertise. However, some questions remain as to how representative their sample is of typical inner-city children, and how representative their results are of *all* children in their sample.

The Brown and Campione FCL program illustrates an elaborate approach to improving students' "comprehension" and application of specific content. As they emphasize, it involves far more than simply adding vocabulary or basic reading skills. They also emphasize that implementing the program is a complex business, and that there is little profit in simply copying *some* of the components of their program. While I strongly support the overall approach taken in the FCL program (see *Nurturing Independent Learners* by Donald Meichenbaum and myself), I suspect that much progress can be achieved in enhancing children's language with some of the simpler interventions described in this and the preceding chapter.

Conclusion

These examples do not resolve the relative merits of more elaborate, discussion-oriented instruction vs. simpler vocabulary-exposure and vocabulary instruction programs. What can be said is that the simpler programs (e.g., Feitelson, Elley) are much less complex, much more likely to be implemented, and seem to produce results of a similar magnitude.

Current school curricula *may* include strategies for identifying new words ("structural analysis") and *may* include reading material with deliberately expanded vocabulary. There is *some* evidence that when these conditions are combined, disadvantaged children gain vocabulary more effectively. Unfortunately, there is also evidence that these conditions are not often met, and that many children are not very effective at building vocabulary simply through reading. It appears that supporting language/vocabulary growth in the later elementary years requires:

- starting with a larger vocabulary base from the earlier primary years;
- teacher attention to "problem" words;
- systematically increasing the vocabulary children are exposed to and use; and
- including some vocabulary strategy instruction and opportunities to use the strategies.

I cannot assert that these principles are completely *proven*, only that there is some evidence which is consistent with these vocabulary learning principles.

Chapter Six

Increasing the Emphasis on Language Development in Elementary School: Problems and Possibilities

Examples from the preceding chapters clearly demonstrate that we can significantly improve the academic achievement of less advantaged and ESL children by raising levels of *listening* comprehension in the primary years and by increasing listening *and reading* comprehension in grades 3 to 6. Specifically, scheduling challenging *oral language* activity for 20 to 30 minutes a day in kindergarten/primary classes, and a half hour a day with challenging *reading or oral language* in the upper elementary grades may be sufficient to add three to five words a day to the children's vocabulary. This will bring the majority of students to language levels at which they can profit from grade-level instruction. The alternative is to continue to accept the marked gap in achievement that exists between advantaged and disadvantaged children. Advantaged children have many opportunities to expand their language outside of school, building on vocabulary and language skills acquired by grade 4. Less advantaged children whose parents and caretakers spend little time talking or reading to them, and whose home and peer environments provide much less opportunity to learn and use new words and language structures, are far less well equipped to profit from the new vocabulary and language which is increasingly introduced in schools from grade 4 on.

For a long time, we have known that reading success means good word identification skills *plus* growth in general *comprehension*, which is largely reflected in vocabulary. The recent "phonics wars" have led to an acknowledgment by virtually all elementary education researchers that phonics skills must be taught. Many researchers agree that phonics skills are better learned when taught in meaningful context which gradually but systematically introduces specific new letter-sound relationships (systematic phonics). This agreement on the need for phonics instruction is reflected in increased program time for phonics, increased sales of phonics-emphasis reading programs, and improving reading scores for children.

The evidence reviewed in this book suggests that at least *one-half* of elementary school children could also benefit substantially from an increased educational emphasis on challenging language. In addition, there should be an emphasis on ensuring that most children acquire a command of *all* grade-level vocabulary plus a proportion of words known by children above their own grade level. (I mean particularly words commonly known by children 1-2 grade levels above a child's own level, and some words beyond that level.)

As with any new proposal in education, teachers will want to know: *when* this increased emphasis on language and vocabulary can be done in a classroom program, by *whom*, and what *part of the current program must be sacrificed?* There are a limited number of hours in the school day, and little evidence that lengthening those hours would lead to further learning.[33] Typically, there are about four hours a day available for instruction after time for recesses, routine tasks, physical education, and other interruptions to a teacher's program is deducted. The question is how best to use these.

A Language Arts Curriculum

Broadly speaking, I suggest that about half of the total teaching time in elementary school should be devoted to language arts, with the other half being divided between mathematics and other topics. In kindergarten, this would mean that children would spend a total of 45 to 60 minutes in planned language arts activities. In the rest of the elementary program, this would mean about two hours devoted to language arts.

What follows is a brief outline of how four daily half-hour periods might be used for literacy instruction in elementary programs (two periods in kindergarten). After summarizing the four periods, I have provided some suggestions for implementing such a curriculum at the kindergarten, primary, and upper elementary levels. My intention is *not* to suggest that all elementary programs should be organized exactly alike, but rather to demonstrate that it is *possible* to incorporate a listening and language comprehension component into the literacy program of a typical elementary school day.

---

[33] I should note, however, that lengthening the school year is a separate consideration. There is much evidence that many children, especially disadvantaged children, "backslide" during the long summer vacation.

Children need about:

- Half an hour of *daily reading skills* instruction
  - *early:* letter identification, phonemic awareness, basic phonics, word identification.
  - *later:* reading more advanced spelling patterns, book structure (contents, index, chapters, etc.).

- Half an hour of *daily reading practice* (actually successfully reading books that are somewhat challenging for students to *read*, with some consistent relationship to reading skills being taught. For example, if a set of letter-sound relationships has been taught, reading material should include numerous examples of these phonic patterns. Some form of word identification assistance may be appropriate. Note that books used during reading *practice* may not be as advanced as those read while working with the teacher. The emphasis must be on successfully reading a lot of text.
  - *early:* basals and child chosen books appropriate to an individual child's *reading* comprehension level; may be somewhat more advanced if reading assistance is available. *Not applicable to most kindergarten children.*
  - *later:* greater emphasis on books that are challenging at a listening or conceptual level. Reading *and* vocabulary assistance available as needed.

- Half an hour of *daily language challenge*: engagement with text that is challenging at the individual child's *listening* comprehension level, and which includes explanation of new words (3-5 per day).
  - *early:* daily language challenge activities must occur in an *oral* context. Before grades 3 or 4, most children's reading skills and reading comprehension fall well below what is challenging oral language for them.
  - *later:* language challenge activities can increasingly be incorporated into general reading activities. *Note, however, that for many children to "keep up," oral (or video) language sources will remain important at least until the end of elementary school.*

- Half an hour of *daily writing skill and strategy instruction and practice.* This includes printing/spelling, and creating simple but meaningful messages, journal entries, reports, and stories. *Not applicable to most kindergarten children.*
  - *early:* daily writing activities must include the mechanics of printing and spelling words as well as constructing written communications.

- *later:* daily writing instruction encompasses different forms/purposes of writing, and strategies for planning/organizing writing, as well as word-processing skills.

Note that this curriculum involves quite different types of content and teacher and student activities for *word identification* and *reading practice* than it does for *language challenge* and *writing instruction*. Chall, Jacobs, and Baldwin stressed this point in *The Reading Crisis* (1990).

Themes or Units. Some aspects of reading practice, language challenge, and writing practice may well be tied into other content "themes." However, it is important to ensure that grade-level vocabulary and reading and writing skills are introduced, taught, and consolidated or practiced during the school year.[34]

Sample Programs

The preceding outline represents a curriculum which can be realistically scheduled during a morning language arts program. However, can one *teacher* implement this program with 20–25 children who vary substantially in their vocabulary knowledge and reading and writing achievement?

There is enough time in a normal school morning (9:00-12:00) for the children to participate in four teaching periods — two before morning recess and two after. With additional time taken up by opening routines, transitions, recess, and possibly a short relaxed story session at the end of the morning,[35] four half-hour periods are available. Not all children need to be in the same learning settings at the same time. Thus some of the time, some children will typically be working independently or with assistance from other children while the teacher works with an instructional group. The following discussion explains how the four language arts periods could realistically be arranged in primary and upper elementary programs (two periods in kindergarten).

---

[34] In my experience, *most* children, including disadvantaged children, know at least half of "grade level" words. Appendix A contains a list of root words that children need to know by grade 4.

[35] I draw a sharp distinction between reading used as a "transition" activity (e.g., to settle children down at the end of morning or beginning of the afternoon — or bedtime for that matter), and reading used as part of the educational curriculum. For "transition," the criteria of success are that all of the children enjoy what is read, and that they "settle down." There is no emphasis on learning. For oral reading as curriculum, teachers should monitor what the children are learning, provide some vocabulary instruction or assistance, and probably tailor material to challenge the comprehension level of the children to some degree.

Kindergarten

I suggest that children participate in two instructional periods in kindergarten: pre-reading skills and language challenge.

Pre-Reading Skills Instruction in kindergarten might particularly emphasize phonological awareness, an understanding that words can be decomposed into sounds. In addition, there should be an introduction to the letters of the alphabet with emphasis on using letters to form important words (e.g., children's names, labels for areas and materials in the room, etc.). Such instruction might occur in small groups for 15 minutes a day (or 3 days a week). Once routines are established, it has been my observation that kindergarten teachers are able to work with one small group while the other children are engaged in learning center activities.

If, by the end of kindergarten, children have become phonologically aware and can name (and possibly print) the letters of the alphabet, they will be well prepared to learn the mechanics of reading (Chall, 1967/1983; Stanovich, Cunningham, & Cramer, 1984; Yopp, 1995).

Daily Language Challenge in kindergarten should include a story period for approximately 20 minutes, and introduce 3 or 4 new words per day from those stories. Stories should probably be repeated several times (either on consecutive days or at spaced intervals). The studies described in the last chapter suggest that the daily language challenge can successfully carried out on a whole-class basis.

There is little evidence to support explicit *writing instruction and reading practice* in kindergarten for *all* children. For example, the results of Durkin's (1970, 1974) early studies of a kindergarten reading and writing program suggested that about *half* of the children made significant progress as a result of formal kindergarten instruction while the others did not. In the absence of stronger data, I would place more emphasis on reading to children and discussion, possibly in small groups, before investing time in accelerating the reading and writing skills of those who would do well anyway.

Primary (with particular focus on first grade)

In first grade, children should participate in all four periods: reading skills, reading practice, language challenge, and writing.

The *Reading Skills Instruction* period could be done in half-class groups. The teacher works on phonics activities with one group, while the other group reads. (See Daily Reading Practice, below). Those working with the teacher would have a relatively short formal lesson, followed by appropriate consolidation or practice activities. (See Jolly Phonics[36] or other effective programs.) As students move into independent phonics assignments, the teacher could join the other students in a reading practice setting for some discussion of what had been read.

The *Daily Reading Practice (and Discussion)* period would occur with word-identification assistance available, either on tape, from a volunteer, or from a more able child (from the same class or a different class). Even with assistance available, children should not be confronted with reading material that introduces more than 5–10% of words that are difficult to read *or* understand. With assistance available, this period should not require the classroom teacher's full-time attention. For the latter part of the period, the teacher might join a sub-group of the class (different groups on alternate days) to discuss what was read. Such discussion, along the lines of Transactional Strategy Instruction or Reciprocal Teaching, would help emphasize that the purpose of reading is understanding the texts, not simply identifying words.

The *Language Challenge* period would involve reading stories to the whole class or to a group of children while providing necessary explanations or clarifications of words. Books should be chosen that introduce the target vocabulary of words known by the majority children by the end of the current grade level, and some words known by children *above* the current grade level. A target vocabulary list for grades K-4 is given in Appendix A. The simplest source of such stories is found in basal readers one to two grade levels above the children's current grade, selected from series other than those used in the school reading program. Many of these readers contain vocabulary guides: listings of words introduced by page and alphabetical order. These readers should introduce 25–35 unfamiliar words a week. If there is a large variation in the vocabulary levels of the children in the class, it may be necessary to work with two different groups of children — those with stronger and weaker vocabulary levels. If books without vocabulary listings are used, the teacher will need to review the books to identify words requiring attention, bearing in mind target vocabulary.[37] It is

---

[36] Jolly Phonics is a program that has been extensively used in Britain and Ontario, Canada. It is discussed in Dale Willows' book in the present series.

[37] It is also possible to list the words in a story alphabetically, using a word processing program. The story must first be scanned, or typed into the word-processing program. (Primary-level stories are usually not very long.) The story can also be analyzed using the Readability Master software offered by Brookline Books. This will list all words above the fourth-grade level. Appendix B provides more information on assessing vocabulary in a text.

also desirable to include some discussion of story or text content and its implications. Opportunities should be provided for generating language, ranging
from games like "Twenty Questions" (perhaps Ten Questions in first grade?),
describing class events, generating and retelling narratives, etc. Such activities
should *not* be restricted to the level of children's writing skills. A similar approach can be used at the second- and third-grade levels, using stories from
readers for the next highest grade.

Traditionally, there has been some suggestion that children must have direct experience with content in order to learn language. However, children
clearly build some associations without direct experience: e.g., *battle, castle, fair-
ies, elves, cows,* etc. These are known only through verbal experience, not direct
experience. Yet children can talk about castles and battles and understand stories about them. Thus words allow a level of "vicarious experience" (Mischel,
1968). We don't want all school experience and learning to be vicarious, but we
would certainly be limiting learning if we restricted all content to "real" or
"experienced" phenomena.

Hopefully, one overall outcome of the language challenge component would
be an increased interest in word knowledge by students, as reflected both in
expanding vocabularies and in increased frequency of questioning unfamiliar
words.

The *Writing Instruction* period would involve direct instruction in writing
letters and spelling words including spelling strategies, once phonics skills begin to be acquired, as well as regular opportunities for meaningful writing. This
instruction might be done on a half-class basis, while the other half carries out
previous writing assignments.

Upper Elementary Grades

Reading Skills Instruction at this level would shift from an emphasis on word
identification skills and understanding of simple punctuation and story structure to an understanding of different kinds of texts and more extended use of
language resources (e.g., dictionaries, library research methods, etc.). However, I
would also include "structural analysis" of words, as illustrated in the Nicol,
Graves, and Slater (1984) paper described in Chapter Five. In her *Stages of Reading Development,* Jeanne Chall describes a shift from "learning to read" to "reading to learn" (1983/1996). Reading tasks would increasingly lead to knowledge
outcomes. The use of varied reading strategies for different purposes (e.g., skim-
ming, reading for detail, etc.) would be introduced, along with discussions of

when such strategies are appropriate. I would also introduce or expand use of computer resources at this point (e.g., Internet, computer databases and other resources, etc.) as well as library research skills. Such reading skills might be covered in groups meeting once or twice a week, and consolidated in the course of classroom and library reading and research.

However, most teachers are well aware that for many children, basic reading skills remain a serious problem in the upper elementary grades. They will require continued instruction in word identification strategies (mostly advanced phonics), either as part of the regular classroom program or in separate instructional settings.

Daily Reading Practice: Studies (Shany & Biemiller, 1995; Cunningham & Stanovich, 1991; Anderson, Wilson, & Fielding, 1988) have demonstrated that higher levels of reading practice in the upper elementary grades are clearly associated with increased reading and language comprehension, and that this is not simply a correlate of possessing better reading skills. In the Shany and Biemiller study, the authors were surprised to learn that students who were reading with assistance for 30 minutes a day read *five to ten times as much total text as comparable classmates* who were not in the reading practice program. Thus a continued emphasis on in-school reading, and the provision of the assistance conditions needed for reading success, appear to be necessary components of a successful literacy program. For the majority of children, we cannot depend on out-of-school reading, nor can we assume that simply declaring a half-hour unrestricted reading period ensures an adequate level of practice. (Such periods were part of the school program for Shany and Biemiller's "control" children, and are a common part of a great many elementary classrooms today.) Many upper elementary children continue to need assistance with word identification when reading grade-level or above-level texts. In addition, they will also need assistance with word meanings.[38]

Daily Language Challenge: For upper elementary children whose reading skills are equal to their listening comprehension level, and whose comprehension level is at grade level or better, the content curriculum (literature, science, and social studies) will provide opportunities to continue expanding their knowledge and language. However, for the *majority* of children whose reading skills and/or language knowledge do not permit them to deal with grade level content books without assistance, it remains important to continue to provide

---

[38] In Shany and Biemiller's study, we did not find many instances of children seeking word meaning support. However, only a few children reached a point of reading material that introduced many new words.

opportunities to build language knowledge above the level of reading skill limitations. This suggests a continuing need to read literature to children that is at their *listening* comprehension levels, in addition to having them read books at their reading levels. We must ensure that new words continue to be steadily added to children's vocabulary.

Much of this daily language challenge can occur in the context of ongoing content area instruction. However, it is important to determine which children will need assistance with content-area reading. This will be a major source of language growth, *if* appropriate assistance can be supplied. It may be desirable to continue reading content area books to all or part of the class, and to continue providing definitions or clarification as needed.

In addition, in the upper elementary grades, some attention to "structural analysis," or ways of determining word meanings using prefixes and suffixes in conjunction with root words, should be part of the program. (See the discussion of Nicol, Graves, and Slater in Chapter Five.)

Daily Writing Skill Instruction and Practice should increasingly be for real purposes (e.g., writing stories for younger children to read, writing reports, newspapers, letters, Internet communications, "journals," etc.) rather than simple exercises.[39] Writing instruction should focus on the purpose of the particular piece being written, and involve organizational strategies (outlining, paragraphs, headings, etc.) which should be related to the overall purpose of the text being written. Editing skills should increasingly be taught and used. In general, writing, like reading, may increasingly occur as part of other activities (e.g., social studies, school newspaper) rather than as an end in itself.

Conclusion

With increasing pressure to teach reading (word identification), mathematics, and science while addressing other social needs (classes with children from many cultures, children with diverse first languages, and increasing numbers of children with problems associated with declining family stability and increasing poverty), the last thing teachers want to hear is a new curriculum expectation around language! Unfortunately, the same social context (increasing poverty, increasing numbers of children from disadvantaged circumstances which

---

[39] It has been fashionable in recent years to suggest that all writing should be "purposeful." I believe that this can be overdone, making genuine "purposeful" writing seem like just another exercise. However, by the upper elementary years, most children have acquired sufficient writing skills to begin to seriously undertake some "authentic" writing tasks.

do not promote high-level comprehension in English) make the importance of an explicit language focus critical.

Let me once again acknowledge that an increased focus on developing vocabulary and listening comprehension will be difficult. Simply *assessing* progress is hard, as such assessment often requires individual oral testing. This is one reason why oral language and listening comprehension have been neglected. However, *not* finding the time to ensure that children know grade-level vocabulary and some post-grade level vocabulary and to ensure that children use language to understand their world, will further aggravate the growing gulf between advantaged and disadvantaged children.

Appendix A

Common Root Words

The following list is derived from the Dale-Chall list of 3000 words commonly known by grade 4. About four-fifths of these words were passed by more than 80% of the grade 4 samples used for Dale and O'Rourke's **Living Word Vocabulary** (1981). This list differs from that given in Chall & Dale (1995) in that only root words are shown. There are approximately 2300 words. Note, however, that these 2300 words are associated with 3970 different meanings known by children under grade 4, or about 1.7 meanings per word. It would be desirable to have most children familiar with most (90%) of the words on this list by the end of grade 2 or 3. Most children who speak English at home will know well over half of these words by the beginning of first grade.

A good short test of student knowledge of the words in this vocabulary list can be constructed by sampling one word from each column in the list, or about 30 words. Make a sentence using each word and ask the child what the word means in that sentence. Responses can be written if the child's writing skills are adequate. (Making the sentences can be a good exercise for children, especially in grades 2 and 3. Have small groups of children make sentences for 5 or 10 words. Each group is then tested using sentences they didn't construct.)

able	adult	alley	appear	at
about	adventure	along	applause	atlas
above	advice	alphabet	apple	August
absent	afraid	amaze	April	aunt
accident	after	America	apron	author
account	again	amount	area	automobile
acid	age	and	arithmetic	autumn
acorn	agree	angel	arm	avenue
across	aid	anger	arrange	award
act	aim	animal	arrive	awful
add	air	ankle	arrow	
address	alarm	answer	art	baa
admire	album	ant	as	baby
adore	all	ape	ask	back

bacon	bib	bow	burn	catsup
bad	Bible	bow-wow	bus	cattle
bag	big	bowl	bush	cause
bait	bill	box	business	cave
bake	billion	boy	but	celebrate
balance	bingo	brace	butter	cent
ball	bird	brain	button	center
banana	birth	branch	buy	cereal
band	bit	brave	buzz	chain
bank	bite	bread	by	chair
bar	black	break		chalk
barber	blank	breast	cabbage	change
bare	blanket	breath	cabin	channel
bark	blast	breeze	cage	charge
barn	blaze	brick	cake	charm
basket	bless	bride	calendar	chase
bat	blind	bridge	call	cheap
bath	blink	bright	camel	cheat
battle	block	bring	camera	check
beach	blond	brook	camp	cheer
beak	blood	broom	can	cheese
beam	bloom	brother	Canada	cherry
bean	blossom	brown	candle	chest
bear	blot	brush	candy	chew
beat	blouse	bubble	cane	chick
beauty	blow	bucket	cannon	chicken
beaver	blue	buckle	canyon	chief
bed	board	bud	cap	child
bee	boat	budge	captain	chili
beef	body	buffalo	car	chill
begin	bomb	bug	care	chimney
belief	bonnet	buggy	carpenter	chimpanzee
bell	boo	build	carpet	chin
belly	book	bulb	carriage	china
belt	boom	bull	carrot	chip
bench	boot	bump	carry	chipmunk
bend	born	bun	cart	chirp
berry	boss	bunch	cartoon	chocolate
best	both	bundle	carve	choke
bet	boulder	bunk	cat	choose
better	bounce	bunny	catch	chop

Church	cookie	daily	ding	ear
church	copy	dairy	dinosaur	early
churn	cord	dam	dirt	earn
circle	cork	damp	dish	earth
circus	corn	dance	dive	east
city	corner	danger	divide	Easter
clap	correct	dare	do	easy
class	cottage	dark	dock	eat
claw	cotton	darling	doctor	edge
clay	count	dart	dog	education
clean	country	dash	doll	egg
climate	course	date	dollar	eight
climb	cousin	daughter	donkey	elastic
clip	cover	day	door	elbow
clock	cow	dead	dope	election
close	cranberry	deal	dot	electricity
cloth	crank	dear	double	elephant
clown	crash	December	down	elevator
coal	crawl	decide	dozen	eleven
coast	crayon	deck	drag	elm
coat	cream	deep	dragon	else
cocktail	creature	deer	drank	empty
cocoa	cricket	defend	draw	encyclopedia
coin	crime	deliver	dream	end
cold	cripple	den	dress	enemy
collar	crisp	dentist	drill	engine
collect	croak	describe	drink	enjoy
college	crook	design	drive	enough
color	crop	destroy	drop	enter
comb	cross	detergent	drown	envelope
come	crow	dial	drowsy	equal
comfort	crowd	dice	drug	errand
comic	cruel	did	drum	escape
comma	crust	die	dry	Eskimo
command	crutch	diet	duck	even
commander	cry	different	dump	evening
complete	cub	difficult	during	ever
cone	cup	dig	dust	every
connect	cut	dim		evil
control		dime	eager	example
cook	dad	dine	eagle	except

exit	fight	frame	gill	grow
explain	file	freckles	giraffe	growl
explore	film	free	girl	guard
explosive	find	freeze	give	guess
expressway	finger	fresh	glad	guest
eye	finish	Friday	glance	guide
	fire	friend	glare	gum
fabulous	first	frog	glass	gun
face	fish	from	globe	gym
fact	fit	front	glove	
factory	five	frost	glow	hail
fade	fix	fruit	glue	half
faint	fizz	fry	go	hall
fair	flag	fudge	goat	ham
fairy	flame	fuel	God	hammer
faith	flap	full	gold	hamster
fall	flash	fun	golf	hand
false	flavor	fur	good	handsome
family	float	furniture	goose	hang
fan	flock	furthest	grab	happen
far	flood		grace	happy
farm	floor	gallon	grade	harbor
fast	flower	gallop	grain	hard
fat	flunk	game	grand	harm
father	flute	gang	grape	harp
favor	fly	garage	grass	harvest
fear	follow	garbage	grave	hat
feast	food	garden	gravel	hate
feather	fool	gargle	gray	have
February	foot	gas	grease	hawk
feed	for	gate	great	hay
feel	force	gather	green	he
feet	forget	gauge	greet	head
fence	fork	gay	grill	health
fern	form	general	grin	hear
festival	fortune	gentle	grind	heart
fever	forty	geography	grip	heat
few	forward	get	grizzly	heaven
fiddle	fountain	giant	groan	heavy
field	four	gift	ground	heel
fifteen	fox	giggle	group	hell

hello	hotel	jacket	kiss	lettuce
helmet	hound	jackpot	kit	level
hen	hour	jail	kitchen	liar
her	house	jam	kitten	library
herd	how	January	knee	lick
here	howl	jar	knife	life
hero	huge	jaw	knight	lift
hi-fi	hum	jay	knit	light
hid	human	jaywalker	knob	lily
high	hundred	jeans	knock	line
hike	hunger	jeep	knot	linen
hill	hunt	jelly	know	lion
him	hurricane	jerk		lip
history	hurry	jet	ladder	liquor
hit	hurt	jewel	lady	list
hitch	husband	job	lake	little
hive	hush	join	lamb	live
ho	hut	joke	lamp	lizard
hobble	hymn	jolly	land	load
hobby		journey	lane	loaf
hockey	ice	joy	language	lobster
hoe	idea	judge	lantern	lock
hold	if	jug	large	log
hole	igloo	juice	last	lollipop
holster	ill	July	late	lone
home	imagine	jump	laugh	long
honey	important	June	laundry	look
honk	impossible	junk	law	loop
honor	in	just	lawn	loose
hood	inch		lazy	Lord
hoof	Indian	kangaroo	leaf	lot
hook	ink	keep	leak	lotion
hoot	inn	ketchup	leap	loud
hop	insect	kettle	learn	love
hope	interfere	key	leave	low
horn	invent	kick	left	luck
horse	invite	kid	leg	luggage
hose	iron	kill	lemon	lullaby
hospital	is	kind	leopard	lumber
hot		kindergarten	less	lunch
hot dog	jack	king	letter	lung

luxury	mess	muffin	nose	page
	message	mule	note	pain
ma	middle	multiply	November	paint
macaroni	midget	mumps	now	pair
machine	mile	murder	number	pajamas
mad	milk	museum	nurse	palace
made	mill	mushroom	nut	pan
magic	mind	music		panda
magnet	mine	mustard	oak	pants
mail	minister	my	oar	paper
man	mink	mystery	obey	parade
manage	minnow		ocean	pardon
mane	mint	name	octopus	parent
many	minute	nap	odd	park
map	miracle	napkin	of	parrot
marble	mirror	narrow	off	part
march	miss	nature	offer	party
March	mister	naughty	office	pass
mark	mitt	navy	often	paste
market	mix	near	oil	pasture
marriage	mob	neat	okay	pat
mash	model	neck	old	patch
mask	moment	need	on	path
match	Monday	needle	one	pave
mate	money	Negro	onion	paw
May	monkey	neighbor	open	pay
maybe	monster	nest	operator	pea
me	moo	net	opossum	peace
meal	moon	new	orange	peach
mean	moose	next	orbit	peacock
measure	mop	nibble	orchard	pear
medicine	morning	nice	order	pecan
meet	motel	nickel	ordinary	peel
melon	moth	night	organ	peep
member	mother	nine	out	pen
memory	motor	no	oven	pencil
mend	mouse	nod	over	penguin
menu	mouth	noise	owl	penny
meow	move	noodle	own	people
mermaid	much	noon		pepper
merry	mud	normal	pack	perfume

perhaps	pole	purple	rest	safe
period	police	purse	restaurant	sail
permit	polite	push	rib	salad
person	pony	put	ribbon	sale
pest	poodle	puzzle	rice	salt
pet	pool		rich	same
phone	poor	quack	riddle	sample
photo	pop	quart	ride	sand
pick	poppy	queen	right	sap
picnic	porch	queer	ring	Saturday
picture	pork	question	rip	save
pie	post	quick	ripe	say
pig	postpone	quiet	river	scale
pigeon	pot	quilt	road	scalp
pile	potato		roar	scamper
pill	pound	rabbit	roast	scare
pillow	pour	raccoon	rob	scatter
pilot	prairie	race	robin	school
pimple	pray	radio	rock	scoop
pin	prepare	radish	rocket	score
pine	present	rag	roll	scratch
ping-pong	press	rail	romance	scream
pink	pretty	rain	roof	screen
pipe	price	raise	root	scrub
pistol	primary	ranch	rope	sea
pit	prince	rang	rose	seal
pitcher	print	range	rot	season
pizza	prison	rascal	rough	seat
place	prize	rat	round	second
plan	program	rattle	route	secret
planet	promise	raw	row	see
plant	proof	reach	royal	seed
plaster	protect	read	rubber	seesaw
plate	proud	ready	rug	sell
play	prove	receive	run	send
plow	puddle	record	rush	September
plum	puff	red	rust	serve
plus	pull	reindeer		seven
pocket	punch	rent	sack	shade
poem	pup	repair	sad	shadow
point	pupil	repeat	saddle	shake

shampoo	sky	sore	state	sun
sharp	slam	sorrow	station	Sunday
shave	slap	soul	statue	sure
she	slave	sound	stay	surgeon
sheep	sled	south	steal	suspect
shepherd	sleep	space	steel	swallow
shine	sleigh	spaghetti	steeple	sweep
ship	slice	spark	step	sweet
shirt	slide	sparrow	stick	swift
shoe	slim	speak	stiff	swim
shoot	slip	spear	still	swing
shop	slosh	speck	sting	switch
shore	slow	speech	stink	sword
short	small	speed	stocking	syllable
shoulder	smart	spend	stone	
shove	smash	spider	stool	table
show	smell	spill	stop	taffy
shy	smog	spin	store	tag
sick	smoke	splash	stork	take
side	snack	split	storm	tale
sight	snail	spool	story	talk
sign	snake	spoon	stove	tall
silence	sneeze	sprain	straight	tame
silk	sniff	spray	strange	tan
sill	snow	spread	strap	tangle
silly	snug	squash	strawberry	tap
silver	so	squeak	stream	tape
sin	soak	squeal	street	tattle
sing	soap	squeeze	strike	tattoo
single	social	squirrel	string	tax
sink	sock	stable	strip	tea
sip	soda	stack	strong	team
sister	soft	stale	studio	teeth
sit	soil	stalk	study	telegram
six	sold	star	stunt	tell
sixty	solid	starch	subtract	tend
size	solve	stare	sudden	tent
skate	some	Stars and	sugar	terrible
skin	son	Stripes	suit	test
skip	song	start	sum	thanksgiving
skunk	soon	starve	summer	theater

their	top	turnip	wake	wing
them	tornado	twenty	walk	wink
then	torpedo	twig	wall	winter
there	total	twist	wallet	wipe
they	touch	two	walnut	wire
thin	toy		wander	wolf
think	trace	ugly	war	woman
third	track	umbrella	warm	wonder
thirst	tractor	uncle	wash	wood
thirty	trade	under	wasp	woof
this	traffic	understand	watch	wool
thousand	trail	United States	water	work
thread	train	up	wave	worm
three	trap	use	wax	wrap
throat	trash		we	wreck
through	travel	vacation	Wednesday	wren
throw	treasure	Valentine	week	wrist
thunder	tree	valley	weigh	write
Thursday	trespass	vanish	went	wrong
ticket	trick	varnish	wheat	
tickle	trip	vase	wheel	yard
tiddlywinks	trombone	vegetable	when	yarn
tie	troop	very	while	yawn
tiger	trophy	vest	whip	year
time	truck	view	whistle	yell
tin	true	visit	white	yellow
tiny	trunk	vitamin	why	yes
tissue	try	voice	wide	young
to	tube	vote	wife	
together	Tuesday		wigwam	zebra
toilet	tug	waffle	wild	zoo
ton	turkey	wagon	win	
too	turn	wait	wind	

Assessing Vocabulary in Children's Books

Books can be informally "graded" by comparing them to standardized passages. Chall, Bissex, Conard, and Harris-Sharples (1996) have described a practical method of making such assessments of literature, science, and social studies books. However, teachers who are interested in identifying the specific vocabulary used in a particular book, or assuring that a known target vocabulary is actually experienced during a year of study, will need a summary of words introduced in that book, and possibly where these words occur.

In our research on fostering vocabulary, my colleagues and I have found that at the primary level, it may be worth simply typing the book out on a regular word processor (e.g., WordPerfect, Word), treating separate chapters or stories as separate documents. Each story or section can then be sorted alphabetically, using the word processor's SORT tool. (This method also indicates how often particular words occur.) While this may seem arduous, the total volume of text covered in most first- and second-grade readers is not actually that great. In books with few pictures, it may also be possible to pick up text through scanning techniques.

I recommend determining whether children are familiar with the root forms of derived words which may appear in the text. (For example, if the word *profitable* appears in the text, establish whether the children know *profit*.) Then note whether they understand *profitable* when it appears. If not, work on suffixes; specifically, the suffix *-able* will be needed.

Those who have Brookline Books' *Readability Master 2000* program can also analyze typed stories using this tool. *Readability Master 2000*'s analyses not only yield estimated grade levels for passages, but also provide lists of words *not* known by the majority of fourth-graders as well as lists *not* known by second-graders. I would suggest that school libraries, parent volunteers, and others might contribute to vocabulary analyses of commonly used school books.

Vocabulary lists thus obtained can be used to check vocabulary knowledge prior to reading or listening to books, gains after experience with books, and comparison to lists of words (or root words) normally known by various grades. I understand that World Book is planning to bring out a CD-ROM version of the *Living Word Vocabulary* in which vocabularies known at specific grades can be listed. At present, such material can only be checked with difficulty in the printed version of the *Living Word Vocabulary* (Dale & O'Rourke, 1981).

References

Adams, A. (1991). The oral reading errors of readers with learning disabilities: Variations produced within the instructional and frustrational ranges. *Remedial and Special Education, 12*(1), 48-55.

Adams, M.J. (1990). *Beginning to read: Thinking and learning about print.* Cambridge, MA: The MIT Press.

Allington, R. (1984). Oral reading. In P.D. Pearson (Ed.), *Handbook of Reading Research* (Vol. 1, pp. 829-864). New York: Longman.

Anderson, R.C., Wilson, P.T., & Fielding, L.G. (1988). Growth in reading and how children spend their time outside of school. *Reading Research Quarterly, 21*, 285-303.

Anderson, R.C. (1996). Research foundations to support wide reading. In V. Greanery (Ed.), *Promoting reading in developing countries.* New York: International Reading Association.

Anglin, J.M. (1977). *Word, object, and conceptual development.* New York: W.W. Norton.

Anglin, J.M. (1993). Vocabulary development: A morphological analysis. *Monographs of the Society for Research in Child Development,* Serial No. 238, *58.*

Arnold, D.H., Lonigan, C.J., Whitehurst, G.J., & Epstein, J.N. (1994). Accelerating language development through picture book reading: Replication and extension to a videotape training format. *Journal of Educational Psychology, 86*(2), 235-243.

Bankson, N.W. (1977). *Bankson Language Screening Test.* Baltimore, MD: University Park Press.

Bates, E., Dale, P.S., & Thal, D. (1995). Individual differences and their implications for theories of language development. In P. Fletcher & B. MacWhinney (Eds.), *Handbook of Child Language* (pp. 96-151). Oxford, UK: Blackwell.

Beck, I., & McKeown, M. (1990). Conditions of vocabulary acquisition. In R. Barr, M.L. Kamil, P.B. Mosenthal, & P.D. Pearson (Eds.), *Handbook of Reading Research,* Vol. 2 (pp. 789-814). New York: Longman.

Beck, I.L., Perfetti, C., & McKeown, M.G. (1982). Effects of long-term vocabulary instruction on lexical access and reading comprehension. *Journal of Educational Psychology, 74*, 506-521.

Becker, W.C. (1977). Teaching reading and language to the disadvantaged: What we have learned from field research. *Harvard Educational Review, 47,* 518-543.

Biemiller, A. (1970). Changes in the use of graphic and contextual information as children learn to read. *Reading Research Quarterly, 6,* 75-96.

Biemiller, A. (1979). Changes in the use of graphic and contextual information as functions of passage difficulty and reading achievement level. *Journal of Reading Behavior, 11,* 307-318.

Biemiller, A. (1994). Some observations on beginning reading instruction. *Educational Psychologist, 29*(4), 203-209.

Biemiller, A. (1998, April). *Oral vocabulary, word identification, and reading comprehension in English second language and English first language elementary school children.* Paper presented at the annual meeting of the Society for the Scientific Study of Reading, San Diego, CA.

Blaxall, J., & Willows, D.M. (1984). Reading ability and text difficulty as influences on second graders' oral reading errors. *Journal of Educational Psychology, 76,* 330-341.

Bloom, B. (1964). *Stability and change in human characteristics.* New York: Wiley.

Bloom, B. (1976). *Human characteristics and school learning.* New York: McGraw-Hill.

Bloom, L. (1998). Language acquisition in its developmental context. In D. Kuhn & R.S. Siegler (Eds.), *Handbook of child psychology* (5th ed.), Vol. 2 (pp. 309-370). New York: Wiley.

Bond, G.L., & Dykstra, R. (1967/1997). The cooperative research program in first-grade reading instruction. *Reading Research Quarterly, 32,* 345-427. (Reprint of the original article which appeared in 1967)

Brown, A.L., & Campione, J.C. (1994). Guided discovery in a community of learners. In K. McGilly (Ed.), *Classroom lessons: Integrating cognitive theory and classroom practice* (pp. 229-272). Cambrige, MA: The MIT Press.

Brown, A.L., & Campione, J.C. (1996). Psychological theory and the design of innovative learning environments: On procedures, principles, and systems. In L. Schauble & R. Glaser (Eds.), *Innovations in learning: New environments for education* (pp. 289-326).

Brown, A.L., & Palincsar, A.S. (1989). Guided, cooperative learning and individual knowledge acquisition. In L.B. Resnick (Ed.), *Knowing, learning, and instruction: Essays in honor of Robert Glaser* (pp. 393-452).

Brown, R., Pressley, M., Van Meter, P., & Schuder, T. (1996). A quasi-experimental validation of transactional strategies instruction with low-achieving second-grade readers. *Journal of Educational Psychology, 88,* 18-37.

Bus, A.G., Van Ijzendoorn, M.H., & Pellegrini, A.D. (1995). Joint book reading makes for success in learning to read: A meta-analysis on intergenerational transmission of literacy. *Review of Educational Research, 65,* 1-21.

Cantalini, M. (1987). *The effects of age and gender on school readiness and school success.* Unpublished doctoral dissertation. Toronto, Canada: Ontario Institute for Studies in Education.

Case, R. (1985). *Intellectual development: Birth to adulthood.* New York: Academic Press.

Case, R., & Okamoto, Y. (1998). The role of central conceptual structures in the development of children's thought. *Monographs of the Society for Research in Child Development,* Serial No. 246, *61.*

Chall, J.S. (1967/1983). *Learning to read: The great debate.* New York: McGraw-Hill.

Chall, J.S., Bissex, G.L., Conard, S.S., & Harris-Sharples, S. (1996). *Qualitative assessment of text difficulty: A practical guide for teachers and writers.* Cambridge, MA: Brookline Books.

Chall, J.S., & Conard, S.S. (1991). *Should textbooks challenge students?* New York: Teachers College Press.

Chall, J.S., & Dale, E. (1995). *Readability revisited: The new Dale-Chall readability formula.* Cambridge, MA: Brookline Books.

Chall, J.S., Jacobs, V.A., & Baldwin, L.E. (1990). *The reading crisis: Why poor children fall behind.* Cambridge, MA: Harvard University Press.

Christie, J.F., & Alonso, P.A. (1980). Effects of passage difficulty on primary-grade children's oral reading error patterns. *Educational Research Quarterly, 5,* 41-49.

Cummins, J. (1985). *Bilingualism in education: Aspects of theory, research, and practice.* New York: Longmans.

Cunningham, A.E., & Stanovich, K.E. (1991). Tracking the unique effects of print exposure in children: Associations with vocabulary, general knowledge, and spelling. *Journal of Educational Psychology, 83*(2), 264-274.

Curtis, M.E. (1980). Development of components of reading skill. *Journal of Educational Psychology, 72,* 656-669.

Dale, E., & O'Rourke, J. (1981). *The living word vocabulary.* Chicago: World Book/Childcraft International.

Dickinson, D.K., & Smith, M.W. (1994). Long-term effects of preschool teachers' book readings on low-income chidlren's vocabulary and story comprehension. *Reading Research Quarterly, 29,* 104-123.

Duncan, G., Brooks-Gunn, J., & Klebanov, P. (1994). Economic deprivation and early childhood development. *Child Development, 65,* 296-318.

Dupuy, H. (1974). The rationale, development, and standardization of a basic word vocabulary test (DHEW Publication No. HRA74-1334). Washington, DC: U.S. Government Printing Office.

Durkin, D. (1970). A language arts program for pre-first grade children: Two year achievement report. *Reading Research Quarterly, 5,* 534-565.

Durkin, D. (1974-1975). A six year study of children who learned to read in school at the age of four. *Reading Research Quarterly, 10,* 9-61.

Durkin, D. (1978). What classroom observations reveal about reading comprehension. *Reading Research Quarterly, 14,* 518-544.

Elley, W.B. (1989). Vocabulary acquisition from listening to stories. *Reading Research Quarterly, 24,* 174-186.

Elshout-Mohr, M., & van Daalen-Kapteijns, M.M. (1987). Cognitive processes in learning word meanings. In M.G. McKeown & M.E. Curtis (Eds.), *The nature of vocabulary acquisition* (pp. 53-72). Hillsdale, NJ: Erlbaum:

Feitelson, D., Goldstein, Z., Iraqi, J., & Share, D.I. (1991). Effects of listening to story reading on aspects of literacy acquisition in a diglossic situation. *Reading Research Quarterly, 28,* 70-79.

Feitelson, D., Kita, B., & Goldstein, Z. (1986). Effects of listening to series stories on first graders' comprehension and use of language. *Research in the Teaching of English, 20,* 339-356.

Fleisher, B.M. (1988). Oral reading cue strategies of better and poorer readers. *Reading Research and Instruction, 27,* 35-50.

Fletcher, P., & MacWhinney, B., Eds. (1995). *The handbook of child language.* Oxford, UK: Basil Blackwell Ltd.

Fraser, C. (in press). Lexical processing strategy use and vocabulary learning through reading. *Studies in Second Language Acquisition.* (to appear in the June, 1999 issue)

Freebody, P., & Anderson, R.C. (1983). Effects of vocabulary difficulty, text cohesion, and schema availability on reading comprehension. *Reading Research Quarterly, 18,* 277-294.

Fry, E. (1989). Reading formulas: Maligned but valid. *Journal of Reading, 32,* 292-297.

Gathercole, S.E., Hitch, G.J., Service, E., & Martin, A.J. (1997). Phonological short-term memory and new word learning in children. *Developmental Psychology, 33,* 966-979.

Gerlai, E. (1987). *The effects of language one and language two proficiencies on learning to read.* Unpublished Ph.D. thesis. Toronto, Canada: University of Toronto.

Gersten, R., & Keating, T. (1987). Long term benefits from direct instruction. *Educational Leadership, 45,* 28-31.

Glasspool, J., & Hutton, G. (1993, August). *Enhancing reading instruction for young boys.* Paper presented at a symposium on Whole Language Instruction at the annual convention of the American Psychological Association, Toronto, Canada.

Goodman, K.S. (1973). Miscues: Windows on the reading process. In K.S. Goodman (Ed.), *Miscue analysis: Application to reading instruction.* Champaign-Urbana, IL: ERIC Clearinghouse of Reading and Communication, N.C.T.E.

Graves, M.F., Juel, C., & Graves, B.B. (1998). *Teaching reading in the 21st century.* Boston, MA: Allyn & Bacon.

Graves, M.F. (in press). A vocabulary program to complement and bolster a middle-grade comprehension program. In B.M. Taylor, P. van den Broek, & M.F. Graves (Eds.), *Reading for meaning: Fostering comprehension in the middle grades.* New York: Teachers College Press.

Hart, B., & Risley, T.R. (1995). *Meaningful differences in the everyday experience of young American children.* Baltimore, MD: Paul H. Brookes Publishing Co.

Kucan, L., & Beck, I.L. (1997). Thinking aloud and reading comprehension research: Inquiry, instruction, and social interaction. *Review of Educational Research, 67,* 271-301.

Liberman, A. (1998, April). *Why the scientific study of reading must probe more deeply into speech*. Address to the Society for the Scientific Study of Reading. San Diego, CA.

Marks, C.B., Doctorow, M.J., & Wittrock, M.C. (1974). Word frequency and reading comprehension. *Journal of Educational Research*, 67, 259-262.

McLloyd, V.C. (1998). Socioeconomic disadvantage and child development. *American Psychologist*, 53, 185-204.

Meichenbaum, D., & Biemiller, A. (1998). *Nurturing independent learners: Helping students take charge of their learning*. Cambridge, MA: Brookline Books.

Mischel, W. (1968). *Personality and assessment*. New York: Wiley.

Miller, G.E. (1985). The effects of general and specific self-instructional training on children's comprehension monitoring performances during reading. *Reading Research Quarterly*, 20, 616-628.

Miller, G.A. (1991). *The science of words*. New York: Scientific American Library.

Morrison, F.J., Williams, M.A., & Massetti, G.M. (1998, April). *The contributions of IQ and schooling to academic achievement*. Paper presented at the Annual Meeting of the Society for the Scientific Study of Reading, San Diego, CA.

Morrow, L.M. (1992). The impact of a literacy-based program on literacy achievement, use of literature, and attitudes of children from minority backgrounds. *Reading Research Quarterly*, 27, 250-275.

Nagy, W.E., Herman, P.A., & Anderson, R.C. (1985). Learning words from context. *Reading Research Quarterly*, 20, 233-253.

Nagy, W.E., & Herman, P.A. (1987). Breadth and depth of vocabulary knowledge: Implications for acquisition and instruction. In M.G. McKeown & M.E. Curtis (Eds.), *The nature of vocabulary acquisition* (pp. 19-36). Hillsdale, NJ: Erlbaum.

Nicol, J.E., Graves, M.F., & Slater, W.H. (1984). *Building vocabulary through prefix instruction*. Unpublished manuscript, Department of Curriculum and Instruction, University of Minnesota, Minneapolis, MN.

Palincsar, A.A., & Brown, A.L. (1984). Reciprocal teaching of comprehension-fostering and monitoring activities. *Cognition and Instruction*, 1, 117-175.

Pressley, M., El-Dinary, P.B., Gaskins, I., Schuder, T., Bergman, M., Almasi, J., & Brown, R. (1992). Beyond direct explanation: Transactional instruction of reading comprehension strategies. *Elementary School Journal*, 92, 513-555.

Robbins, C., & Ehri, L.C. (1994). Reading storybooks to kindergartners helps them learn new vocabulary words. *Journal of Educational Psychology*, 86, 54-64.

Rosenshine, B., & Meister, C. (1994). Reciprocal teaching: A review of the research. *Review of Educational Research*, 64, 479-530.

Shany, M., & Biemiller, A. (1995). Assisted reading practice: Effects on performance for poor readers in grades 3 and 4. *Reading Research Quarterly*, 30, 382-395.

Stahl, S., & Fairbanks, M.M. (1986). The effects of vocabulary instruction: A model-based meta-analysis. *Review of Educational Research*, 56, 72-110.

Stanovich, K.E. (1986) Matthew effects in reading: Some implications of individual differences in the acquisition of literacy. *Reading Research Quarterly*, 21, 360-406.

Stanovich, K.E., Cunningham, A.E., & Cramer, B.B. (1984). Assessing phonological awareness in kindergarten children: Issues of task comparability. *Journal of Experimental Child Psychology*, 38, 175-190.

Snow, C. (1996). Issues in the study of input: Finetuning, universality, individual and developmental differences, and necessary causes. In P. Fletcher & B. MacWhinney (Eds.), *Handbook of child language* (pp 180-193). Oxford, UK: Blackwell.

Sternberg, R.J. (1987). Most vocabulary is learned from context. In M.G. McKeown & M.E. Curtis (Eds.), *The nature of vocabulary acquisition* (89-106). Hillsdale, NJ: Erlbaum.

Stone, C.A. (1998). The metaphor of scaffolding: Its utility for the field of learning disabilities. *Journal of Learnng Disabilities*, 31, 344-364.

Tamor, L. (1981). Subjective text difficulty: An alternative approach to defining the difficulty level of written text. *Journal of Reading Behavior, 13*, 165-172.

Templin, M.C. (1957). *Certain language skills in children.* Minneapolis: University of Minnesota Press. (Cited in Beck & McKeown, 1991.)

Tizard, B., Cooperman, O., Joseph, A., & Tizard, J. (1972). Environmental effects on language development: A study of young children in long-stay residential nurseries. *Child Development, 43*, 337-358.

Tizard, B. (1973). Do social relationships affect language development? In K. Connolly & J. Bruner (Eds.), *The growth of competence* (pp. 227-240). New York: Academic Press

Valdes, G. (1998) The world outside and inside schools: Language and immigrant children. *Educational Researcher, 27*, 4-18.

Werner, H., & Kaplan, B. (1952). The acquisition of word meanings: A developmental study. *Monographs of the Society for Research in Child Development, 15*, (Serial No. 51, No. 1).

Wells, C.G. (1985). Language development in the preschool years. New York: Cambridge University Press.

White, B.L., & Watts, J.C. (1973). *Experience and environment.* Englewood Cliffs, NJ: Prentice-Hall.

White, T.G., Power, M.A., & White, S. (1989). Morphological analysis: Implications for teaching and understanding vocabulary growth. *Reading Research Quarterly, 24*, 283-304.

Whitehurst, G.J. (1990). *The Stony Brook emergent literacy curriculum.* Stony Brook, NY: Author. (address: Dr. G.J. Whitehurst, Department of Psychology, State University of New York at Stony Brook, Stony Brook, NY.)

Whitehurst, G.J., Arnold, D.S., Epstein, J.N., Angell, A.L., Smith, M., & Fischel, J.E. (1994). A picture book reading intervention in day care and home for children from low-income families. *Developmental Psychology, 30*, 679-689.

Whitehurst, G.J., Falco, F.L., Lonigan, C., Fischel, J.E., DeBaryshe, B.D., Valdez-Menchaca, M.C., & Caulfield, M. (1988). Accelerating language development through picture book reading. *Developmental Psychology, 24*, 552-588.

Wittrock, M.C., Marks, C.B., & Doctorow, M.J. (1975). Reading as a generative process. *Journal of Educational Psychology, 67*, 484-489.

Wixson, K.L. (1979). Miscue analysis: A critical review. *Journal of Reading Behavior, 11*, 163-175.

Wright, E.N., Kane, T., & Desoran, (1976). *Every student survey: Students' background and its relation to program placement.* Toronto, ON: Toronto Board of Education, Report # 36.

Yopp, H.K. (1995). A test for assessing phonemic awareness in young children. *The Reading Teacher, 49*(1), 20-29.

About the Author

Andrew Biemiller has been studying reading and education since his doctoral work in Project Literacy at Cornell University in the 1960s. As both a teacher educator and a researcher at the University of Toronto, he has been involved with classroom practices and realities for over 30 years. He is currently principal investigator on a three-year study of language assessment and teaching in elementary schools.